New Voices of the Commonwealth

New Voices of the Commonwealth

Edited by Howard Sergeant

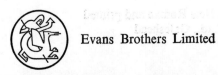

Evans Brothers Limited

Published by Evans Brothers Limited
Montague House, Russell Square, London, W.C.1.

First published 1968

Set in 10 on 11 point Times New Roman and printed
by Northumberland Press Ltd., Gateshead
237 49814 6 PB PR 4779
237 49815 4 CSD

Contents

Introduction

One of the difficulties in writing about Commonwealth poetry is that the Commonwealth itself is in such a constant state of change. The literary commentator or critic cannot be certain that, by the time his observations appear in a printed volume, all the countries to which he may wish to refer will still be members of the Commonwealth, or that new members will not have been introduced in the meantime. For instance, during the course of collecting the poems for this anthology and preparing the volume for publication, what was previously known as British Guiana has been given independence under the name of Guyana; India and Pakistan have been involved in a war which was concluded by the Tashkent agreement; Rhodesia has issued U.D.I.—in itself a cause of controversy amongst other members of the Commonwealth—Singapore, though remaining in the Commonwealth, has withdrawn from Malaysia; there have been military coups in both Ghana and Nigeria which have effected a radical change of government, and there have also been serious disturbances in other African countries.

Another problem is that of deciding the nationality of the individual poets. Some poets are born in one part of the Commonwealth and spend most of their lives in another. Others travel widely, perhaps from one university to another, and still maintain a strong personal link with their country of origin. Others identify themselves so clearly with their adopted countries as to effect a change of nationality for all practical purposes. If South Africa withdrew from the Commonwealth a few years ago, a number of South African poets have deliberately chosen to live in Commonwealth countries, and should rightly be regarded as citizens of the Commonwealth.

Although during the last few years there has been a lively and rapidly increasing interest in the poetry written by Commonwealth poets, the term Commonwealth poetry is somewhat difficult to define. We may find that we enjoy the poetry produced in Australia, Canada, or, indeed, any of the English-speaking countries, and it may prove exciting to follow the developments actually taking place in the countries which have gained their independence since the war; yet the poetic output of all these countries making up the Commonwealth can hardly be said to constitute a unified body of poetry in quite the same sense that all the poetry produced in the United States constitutes an

American poetry. Nor would it be desirable. For each of the countries involved has its own cultural, economic, social and political problems to tackle in its own way, regardless of what is happening elsewhere. So far as poetic traditions are concerned, they are all at different stages of development, and some of them —notably the African countries—have rich oral traditions, as yet practically untapped. In some of these countries English is the sole language, while in others it is spoken only by sections of the community at present. Some have been self-governing for many years, and others, such as Guyana, have but recently become independent.

What all these countries have in common, however, in greater or less degree, is the English language; and since, in each case, the tensions, pressures, sensibilities, customs and traditions are different, so will their use of English be different. It is in the belief that this is already beginning to prove the case that this anthology has been compiled. 'The English language,' says Professor R. K. Narayan (in *Commonwealth Literature*), 'through sheer resilience and mobility, is now undergoing a process of Indianization in the same manner as it adopted U.S. citizenship over a century ago, with the difference that it is the major language there but here one of the fifteen listed in the Indian constitution.' 'As is to be expected' writes J. O. Ekpenyong (of the University of Nigeria), 'the use of English in Nigeria is quite characteristic and different from English as used in the United Kingdom and in the United States. An important factor responsible for the difference is cross-association of speech patterns or the interference of the mother tongue of the Nigerian with his English.'

It has, in fact, been observed by a number of reliable authorities on the subject that poetry in English is already taking on new dimensions as a result of this process. Each of the Commonwealth countries is beginning to use the language in its own particular way. Since the historical developments of Australian, Canadian and New Zealand poetry have already been studied at length by competent critics, and some admirable collections of the poetry of individual Commonwealth countries are now available, the most important function of any anthology devoted to Commonwealth poetry as a whole is to provide examples of the work produced in all the countries which comprise the Commonwealth and to set them against a common background for comparison and assessment. Only in this way can we judge the extent to which each of these countries is beginning to make its own contributions to English literature in general; and perhaps we shall be able to discern the trends and directions, such as they may be, most clearly of all by listening to the 'New Voices' of the Commonwealth.

Here, for instance, is the voice of Kwesi Brew of Ghana:
'They could not silence the drums,

The fibre of their souls and ours—
The drums that whisper to us behind black sinewy hands.'

and here that of Neville Dawes of the West Indies:
'Have seen the summer convex of the wounded sky
want to catch it and clutch it and make it sing
of the wild wind's whisper and the hard-boiled sun. . . .'

In *Once Upon a Time* Gabriel Okara (Nigeria) deals with an
experience recognizable to all of us, though he uses his own form
of expression:

'So I have learned many things, son.
I have learned to wear many faces
like dresses—homeface,
officeface, streetface, hostface, cock-
tailface, with all their conforming smiles
like a fixed portrait smile . . .'

but in *The Mystic Drum,* on the other hand, he draws upon the
African tradition:

'Then the drum beat with the rhythm
of the things of the ground
and invoked the eye of the sky
the sun and the moon and the river gods—
and the trees began to dance,
the fishes turned men
and men turned fishes
and things stopped to grow. . . .'

Local colour is to be discerned in such poems as *The Singing
Bones* by Randolph Stow, *The Dry Season* by Kwesi Brew,
Night of the Scorpion by Nissim Ezekiel, *An African Thunder-
storm* by David Rubadiri, *Grafton Bridge* by Mark Young, and
They Walked and Talked by C. Uche Okeke, and many other
poems in this collection.
We may find it interesting to compare the different types of
imagery employed by the poets as a result of their particular
experience in a particular society situated in a particular part
of the world. In *Night Rain* John Pepper Clark (Nigeria) adopts
a local image to describe the effect of water seeping through the
roof, as his mother rescues

'. . . . her bins, bags, and vats
Out of the run of water
That like ants filing out of the wood
Will scatter and gain possession
Of the floor. . . .'

13

but it helps us to visualize the scene more clearly; while Thomas Shapcott (Australia) presents an entirely different aspect of water in his *Water Skier*:

'Water fans apart and gasps
beneath the skier's blade-swift skill
and even the river's wading reeds
gasp semaphores of praise at all

this rippling youth's display and ease.'

Still another picture is provided by Mohamad Haji Salleh (Malaysia and Singapore):

'When the rain broadcasts the glass face of the fields
    and moves the tidemark of the canals.'

Khadambi Asalache (Kenya) refers to people who tend to sit on the fence rather than commit themselves as 'chameleons wearing weatherproof suits, made to measure'; and Gaminin Seneviratne (Ceylon) writes of heavy machinery 'sprouting lilies in the sky'. The poets of Australia, Canada, New Zealand and the United Kingdom make greater play with urban landscape and imagery, as might be expected, and there is a strong resemblance in tone and attitude between Margaret Atwood's *The City Planners*—

'the houses in pedantic rows, the planted
sanitary trees, assert
levelness of surface like a rebuke
to the dent in our car door. . . .'

and Edwin Brock's satirical *Song of the Battery Hen*—

'You can tell me: if you come by
the North door, I am in the twelfth pen
on the left-hand side of the third row
from the floor: and in that pen
I am usually the middle one of three . . .'

though ostensibly the poems are about different subjects.

Yet, despite the individual use of language and image, metaphor and rhythmic structure, it will be found that many of these poets in various parts of the world have a curious affinity, and often share a peculiarly modern outlook. To lay undue stress upon diction, local colour or imagery, however exciting they may be, would be to create a false impression, and perhaps to miss the real value of the poetry. If we read Commonwealth poems 'less for what they say than for how they use English to say it'. as we have been advised by Dr. Donald Davie (*New Statesman*, 10th Dec. 1965), we shall look only for novelty, strangeness,

14

and even awkwardness of expression. For though it may be convenient for the purpose of analysis to isolate particular elements for discussion, a poem is an organic whole; its form, rhythm, language and pattern are inseparable from its content and meaning. However individually the African, Indian, Pakistani and Caribbean poets may use the English language, they are each of them concerned with the communication of a peculiar experience.

It should be kept in mind that few nations ever succeed in developing a culture entirely from native elements; the English, whose literature has been enriched for centuries by European and American influences, and is now being invigorated by the best Commonwealth writing, perhaps least of all. It would be difficult to estimate our national debt to the Latin and Greek, French, Italian and German languages. The Bible alone has had an incalculable effect. As I have observed on a number of occasions (and it will bear repetition for the sake of emphasis), the culture of every people usually comprises two distinct elements, the regional and the cosmopolitan; and in the course of time these elements blend to constitute the national tradition. Sometimes the process can be seen in operation in the work of a single poet. Christopher Okigbo, John Pepper Clark and Wole Soyinka are all cases in point, to take only Nigeria as an example. In Okigbo's *Distances* we can see the merging of old and new, of personal and universal, of the African and the Western world. Only by stressing and affirming what is most significant in regional, local and communal life, will humanity be able to meet the challenge of the planetary. It is the indigenous outlook and feeling which makes the best of the Commonwealth writers poets of the universal.

Since there are still a few people who confuse regionalism with a provincialism that is largely concerned with the adulation of local scenery and the preservation of local dialects and customs, perhaps I should make it clear that, far from being a redirection to an obsolete past, true regionalism looks to a future in which an organic pattern of everyday life in each community is the source of human dignity and mutual respect. Usually it arises from a natural attachment, conscious or unconscious, to a particular environment; but it may also assert itself in the form of a reaction against social, economic or racial conditions. It finds an outlet through the language, traditional culture and manner of life of the people belonging to the region (even long after they have left the area); always modified, of course, by the emotional and intellectual experience of the individual. To secure and maintain such a balanced state of society, in which each region makes its own contribution to the culture of the nation, or comity of nations, it follows logically that all the complexities of economic, industrial and international relationships must be taken into account. The poet who in his creative activities fails to do so may easily find himself isolated in a 15 mental backwater, at best a local-colourist, at worst a sentimentalist relying solely upon his conception of the past. Internationalism, then, is merely the integration of a diversity of cultures such as can be seen within the Commonwealth.

'Every nation that exists as a self-communing entity requires a mythology of some kind; when such a thing is not inherited, something must be done to create it,' observed the Australian critic, Brian Elliott—a statement which one tends to accept as a generalization until its truth is driven home when one sees it at work in the actual growth of a country's literature. It is this need for a mythology capable of expressing the history, characteristics and potentialities of a people growing into a distinct nationhood, that has compelled the recent developments in the poetry of the Commonwealth countries. The poets of the Commonwealth are beginning to create their own cultural traditions.

In countries like Australia, Canada and New Zealand, we shall find it reflected in such poems as *The Kelly Show* by Charles Higham and *Leichardt in the Desert* by Keith Harrison; in the West Indies by such poems as *Jou'vert* by Edward Brathwaite and *Columbus* by Vivian Virtue; in India and Pakistan there are rich classical traditions to draw upon; and in the African countries there is a vast wealth of oral literature in drum and praise poetry, folklore, narratives, legend and proverbs which, in the words of Chinua Achebe, lie 'like dormant seeds in the dry-season earth, waiting for rain.'

My aim in compiling this anthology of poems, then, is to call attention to the 'new voices' of the Commonwealth; but it will no doubt be appreciated that such an aim creates a further set of problems for the anthologist, since what will be new to one reader will certainly not be new to another. Nor can any hard-and-fast rules be applied in determining what is new in particular countries. Many of the collections of poetry published in India, Pakistan, Africa and the West Indies, for instance, do not reach other countries, so that poets who may have been writing for years and who enjoy considerable reputations in their own countries, may be relatively unknown in other countries. Frank Collymore, of Barbados, is a case in point; and other names will spring readily to the minds of those who have travelled widely or kept closely in touch with Commonwealth developments. The situation for poets of the older countries, on the other hand, is much more favourable. In the United Kingdom—and to a lesser extent in Australia, Canada and New Zealand—so much is being offered by way of grants, prizes and awards to poets, and so much poetry is being published, broadcast, recorded on tape, or read at recitals of one kind or another, that poets achieve recognition at a very early stage of their careers.

So far as the poets of Australia, Canada, New Zealand and the United Kingdom are concerned, I have, therefore, confined my choice to poets who remain unpublished in collected form or who have published no more than one or two volumes. For the poets of the other countries of the Commonwealth, I have made my selection on the basis of recognition outside the country of origin or residence, quite regardless of age or number of local publications, in the hope that the anthology itself will serve to redress some of the anomalies which it may bring to light in this way.

'The existing monuments form an ideal order among themselves, which is modified by the introduction of the new work of art among them,' said T. S. Eliot. If the present rate of development in the countries of the Commonwealth continues, it will not be long before the poetry of the younger nations, written in English, is having a direct influence upon that of the older nations. What may have been backwaters in the past are being transformed into powerful new tributaries to the main stream of English poetry. Whether or not such work will be significant enough to disturb the 'whole existing order' and 'readjust the values of each work of art towards the whole' yet remains to be seen.

HOWARD SERGEANT.

Bruce Beaver

To a Ferry Musician

When every wave was twice as large
As life and threatened worse than death
To frightened boys on ferry trips,
You loomed benign beside your bass,
Bowing and singing under your breath,
Smiling at the likes of us
Made for sudden winks and quips.

Familiar as Saint Christopher,
You found the holy child in us,
And traversing your deeper stream,
Carried all before the day,
Lifting without any fuss
The bother of our being there,
Turning the nightmare into dream.

You took me once beneath your heart
And set my hand upon the bow;
Smothered in rosin, calm with love,
I stroked the hymning wood and heard
You telling it the why and how
My tickling of its ribs offset
The chuckles coming from above.

Then saint and child and instrument
Were played upon by wind and wave
And felt the grave untroubled pulse
Of earth and ocean, fire and air,
Beyond the heart worn on the sleeve
Of weather, faced the depths and saw
Joy walking on the waters there.

But now my praise falls short of life
And stammers in the face of death.
I cannot find you as I would,
An aged comforter of youth;
My only image is a wreath
Of sounds, of chuckling leaves and hum
Of hiving notes to catch a mood.

Slowly the dark bass glides away
Singing before and in your wake,
A giant swan; while from the prow
Smiling and winking at the fares
Who crouch about the stern and quake,

19

You scatter rosin like a rain
And pollinate the dreaming bow.

David Campbell

Windy Gap

As I was going through Windy Gap
A hawk and a cloud hung over the map.

The land lay bare and the wind blew loud
And the hawk cried out from the heart of the cloud,

'Before I fold my wings in sleep
I'll pick the bones of your travelling sheep,

For the leaves blow black and the wintry sun
Shows the trees' white skeleton.'

A magpie sat in the tree's high top
Singing a song on Windy Gap

That streamed far down to the plain below
Like a shaft of light from a high window.

From the bending tree he sang aloud
And the sun shone out of the heart of the cloud

And it seemed to me as we travelled through
That my sheep were the notes that trumpet blew.

And so I sing this song of praise
For travelling sheep and blowing days.

Laurence Collinson

The Sea and the Tiger

The sea sucks in the traveller,
indifferent to his frantic thought;
no more vindictive than a stone
it yet destroys the mite it caught.

The craving tiger seeks no man
where animal will do instead;
it cares not what the flesh be from,
nor whether living, whether dead.

And friends, who plan no cruelty,
without deliberation rise
and drown me with their deeds, and with
their honest mouths eat out my eyes.

James Cowan

In Praise of Sea

By intention came those angry waters,
torn by the wind into pillars subsiding
upon the sand like sugar exploding
between two fingers of sand.

Swift green whirlpools browse the shallows;
strange mechanism of the deep implying
an aqueous crucifix now declining
to a darkly moving tomb.

White gulls weave a pattern of wonder
upon the new blue motionless awakening,
their harsh cries in idle agony acclaiming
dawn dispersing to day.

Sky and sea announce the horizon
before the ears of the eye are hearing
a soundless crash of the two when fusing
by day, in bold communion.

Wrenched sea-weed drifts over the dunes
like coloured streamers thrown when leaving
by ship, to strange places in search of a meaning
to the delight of dreaming alone,

while the wind and waves roar in silence
and the air is dense with salt sea flying
to mythical pinnacles, a rainbow rising
beyond the glint of the sun.

Bruce Dawe

How to go on Not Looking

How to go on not looking
despite every inducement to the contrary,

How to train the dumb elephant, patience,
to balance by command on its circus stool
without betraying its inward teetering,

How to subdue the snarling circle of ifs
by whip-crack, chair-twirl, seeming to look each steadily
in the eye while declining to unwrap
the deadly golden bonbons of their hate,

How to forget also the silence
tenting itself over the old once wildly-applauded acts,
over Beppo and Toni, the Heavenly Twins,
not to mention Bucephalus, the Wonder Horse,

How to cry 'Ladies and Gentle men!' to an empty marquee
where only the canvas flaps in the night wind,
how to people the vacant benches without bitterness,

And how to go on not looking and not looking
until the good years, the good pitches
return and the crowds gasp again
at the recurrent miracle of the balancing elephant,
the dutiful big cats, the Heavenly Twins
making it all look too easy, the ring-master
merely an accessory after the fact.

Bruce Dawe

Abandonment of Autos

'The City Council is reported to be concerned about the number of
old cars being abandoned in city streets,' News Item.

Something about the idea
Appeals to me immensely—the driver
Pulling up in some busy street, after

(A wry touch) manoeuvring dexterously
For a parking-spot, applying the hand-brake,
Stepping out and closing the car-door
For the last time with grave tenderness . . .
There is a rightness
About the farewell scene
Which junk and wrecking-yards
Could never have. In place of the customary
Abject submission to the cold appraisal
Of the merchant as of a mortuary attendant
For whom an old heap is only an inventory of parts
(Working and non-working) there is in this
Seemingly casual walking away from the parked car
(Who is to know that he will not return?)
A largeness of gesture, satisfaction of a
Ramshackle sense of gallantry in circumstances where
Sharp-faced men are forever lifting the bonnet up with a frown,
Disdainfully kicking the tyres,
Discovering a leak in the radiator and offering,
In consequence, next-to-nothing.
It is the urban Arab's Farewell To His Steed,
Down to the final affectionate pat
On the near mudguard before turning away
To shoulder a passage through the indifferent crowds,
Made free in the moment of loss, the one true test,
Only the licence-plate which he carried with him
Into the new life stating as clearly
As any letter of recommendation:
"He is a man who senses the fitness of things."

Rodney Hall

The Invaders

(for George Johnston and Charmian Clift)

For all we can tell they rode upon asses;
an ass no doubt has a kind of dignity—
the sidesaddled brigand, debtor to harvest
with grain in each dangling boot.

Or they might have advanced in bullock carts,
stacking their weapons and loot inside,
lounging with insolent bone-shaken comfort
spitting at dusty strangers.

They might never have owned such beasts at all,
nor even the poorest of wagons or saddles
(just goats for milking, for meat in camp)
no caravan wealth, no silk.

But we with our sympathies mount them on horseback
—in fear as in love demanding vitality—
deck them and bead them with black leather helmets
and whip them to nightmare speed.

Rodney Hall

The Two of Them are Rivals

The two of them are rivals
both attempt the chute of wind,
forcing their climb with flattened hair
toward some exploration of success.
And yet they stay together:
not quarrelling (as most outsiders would expect,
as hydra-headed third men definitely hope)
but edging upward with each other's help
already dangerously above the city.

Painstakingly they rise, at least
one heel between them squarely shouldered
by a plinth of insubstantial sky,
faces streaming with the tide of air;
they yearn to break that wide surface,
free the explosion of their lungs
and suck new brilliance for their blood.
A stunt for stylitists? Acrobats?
Perhaps it is—

but these are also angels of a kind,
now leaping up on mare's-tails
in defiance of the laws of gravitation,
now tripping over nimbus and dangling head down
one toe wedged in the wrack of unfallen hail.
Yet they seldom tumble far
and spare a competence of strength
to lend each other in emergency.
There must be some divinity in such discipline.

Keith Harrison

Leichardt in the Desert

Ludwig Leichardt—the model for Patrick White's novel 'Voss'—
was a nineteenth-century German explorer who died while trying to
cross the Australian desert with a small party.

I did not choose to make this westward journey
Into the dry rock country of the dead
Where in the torpid light the lizards
Flick from our tracks into the mean rock shadows;
To slash that tunnel through the mountain forest,
Cross the grasslands, wade the inland rivers—
I did not choose; say rather I was called
By a voice that followed in restricted
Avenues, stopped me in doubt before my window;
Grew louder, more insistent—till I came.

And now our sullen band proceeds
Into a wilderness of sand and hard-leaved bushes.
We have turned from the cities of our birth:
We spit on the memory of those violent cities;
And we are bound in a hate that has no symbol,
Hating each other's sickness in ourselves.
Our feet kick dust, the whitened bones of animals,
And of men, and our expressionless eyes
Gaze toward the distant dragon-back of mountains
Which is perhaps our destination—
And that thought racks us with a marvellous fear.

I do not know these men. I shall preserve
The strangeness. That way, control.
Hate, sorrow, fear: these three unite us.

Bronze light beating on the gibber plain;
Dust in the mouth. Dreaming of coastal rivers,
The wheeling of the hawk; haunted by images
I must destroy, of lushness, plenitude—vines
Latticed with mellowing light. The mind's profligacy . . .

You mad saints who claim to know this place
Make prayers for those on a dry journey:
Pray that our arrogance does not fail
In this hard light, in this astringent beauty.

Gwen Harwood

New Music

Who can grasp for the first time
these notes hurled into empty space?
Suddenly a tormenting nerve
affronts the fellowship of cells.
Who can tell for the first time
if it is love or pain he feels,
violence or tenderness that calls
plain objects by outrageous names

and strikes new sound from the old names?
At the service of a human vision,
not symbols, but strange presences
defining a transparent void,
these notes beckon the mind to move
out of the smiling context of
what's known; and what can guide it is
neither wisdom nor power, but love.

Who but a fool would enter these
regions of being with no name?
Secure among their towering junk
the wise and powerful congregate
fitting old shapes to old ideas,
rocked by their classical harmonies
in living sleep. The beggars' stumps
bang on the stones. Nothing will change.

Unless, wakeful with questioning,
some mind beats on necessity,
and being unanswered learns to bear
emptiness like a wound that no
word but its own can mend; and finds
a new imperative to summon
a world out of unmeasured darkness
pierced by a brilliant nerve of sound.

Charles Higham

Sand

You can make castles of it, construct
The flying buttresses, gold cannons, where
Wind beats down from the sad Pacific—

Make the tall walls elegant and straight,
Carve slits to watch through as the army comes
With stealthy tread across the white, ribbed strand.

Set on the top a thin and tossing flag—
Let it crack bravely like a gun's report
Snapping straight, its linen pressed by breeze

And put the writhing seahorses down
On the drawbridge made of bits of wood from a ship—
Dig out an even moat for the sea to gurgle in.

And finally, when at dusk after a day of labor
You are done, stand naked in the centre,
The only time you can be a warrior—

Braving the sea's clashing shields to ride
You down, your gawk arms raw, a rusted spade
Clutched in your hand, and a drum of heat

Rapped in your chest till the bold green quiets it.

Charles Higham

The Kelly Show

The bouquet has mimosas, orchids, roses.
She smiles and gathers handfuls of applause;
Propped on the gallows-steps poor Ned composes
A final plea to make his killers pause;
Her womanhood is offered to the people,
His manhood's buckled under by the laws.
One iron bell bangs from the crooked steeple.

She simpers. He, thin, graceless, penitent,
Stares at the hood, the buckle, the cold drop;
Her eyelids flutter still a weak dissent;

27

She starts to think the show may be a flop,
And hooks her skirts up to attentive smiles,
Thinks of the serpent, starts to whisper slop;
He gazes on the sparkling Summer tiles.

It is her brother, bowing at her side,
It's he who shares her calm eclectic grace.
Because he stole the harness for the ride
She lets him steal the thunder from her face,
And, shadowed, watches cheers break over Jim.
But she can hear the manacles' disgrace
Clacking as Kelly retches to the hymn.

For it, she knew, had been a huge mistake:
Glenrowan was his sacrifice and splendour.
He could have vanished in a thorny brake,
And left his kin to make a grey surrender;
But chose to cling there to the exeunt,
Let fall the iron helmet like a fender,
Lift up an eye unquarrelling and blunt.

The curtain falls: she waves a final hand.
He quotes his jot of evidence; he treads
Into the proper place; his smile is bland.
Applause demands her curtsey into beds,
And so she lewdly nods her short assent.
He drops and twists: the watchers nod their heads
And write his name upon the continent.

Evan Jones

Noah's Song

The animals are silent in the hold,
Only the lion coughing in the dark
As in my ageing arms once more I fold
My mistress and the mistress of the Ark.

That, the rain, and the lapping of the sea:
Too many years have brought me to this boat
Where days swim by with such monotony,
Days of the fox, the lion and the goat.

Her breathing and the slow beat of the clock
Accentuate the stillness of the room,
Whose walls and floor and ceiling seem to lock
Into a space as single as the tomb.

A single room set up against the night,
The hold of animals, and nothing more:
For any further world is out of sight—
There are no people, and there is no shore.

True, the time passes in unbroken peace:
To some, no doubt, this Ark would seem a haven.
But all that I can hope for is release.
Tomorrow I'll send out for the dove and raven.

Evan Jones

Boxing On

When the bell rings you come out feeling wary,
Knowing yourself you lack that brilliant snap.
Things change: you've lost your old need to be lairy,
And when the opening comes you see a trap.

You're mad with craft: even your slightest move
Has years of it, each step, each feinting lead
As smooth as when there's weight behind the glove;
You box with shadows just to keep up speed.

It hurts much more now when you're really hit,
But years of training never let it show:
Shocked in your stance, you give no sign of it
But moving in to clinch and hitting low,

You smile for cameramen who call you Kid
(Seen from the right, you're hardly marked at all)
And make with jokes, large gestures where you hid
The years of clipping marking every fall.

At thirty you're already getting old—
Time to hang up the gloves? That's time to kill,
Say twenty years: I'd rather take it cold,
And when I have to then I guess I will.

Christopher Koch

Half-Heard

On the road through the hills I thought I heard it,
Something moving, coming with evening,
In its slow warm breathing through the paddock-land.
The few and spiteful houses there ignored it.

It had come from the coast. I stood on the coast,
Where gulls cried angrily for something that moved
In the sun-plains across the sea.
The water there was heavy with its hand.

And one by one the evening waves caressed the sullen sand.
Quietly they pondered on nothing at all,
On the laying of their long quiet hands, perhaps,
Upon the waiting beach.

Considering carefully nothing at all,
They too ignored the bird's half baffled cry.

Geoffrey Lehmann

Lines for the End of an Era

Canute, knowing that defeat was certain
Still dared the sea. A lesser man
Would have gone hunting or played cards,
Shrugging, 'How can I stop the tide?'
Fools would have bragged the waves would scuttle
At a mere gesture of their sceptres.
But he was brave in his death-knowledge.

Picture the scene. Expensive pennants,
Silk drapes, divans and velvet cushions
Spotted with spray and drying brine
As the waves creep towards the throne
And lap around the courtiers' ankles.
The mastiffs of the king, disturbed,
Pacing in the unearthly calm,
Bark at grey sky and greyer waves,
And the old king sees his own doom,
And all mankind's, yet still sits on.

Geoffrey Lehmann

A Voyage of Lions

Sea-water stained with lion's blood.
Our arrows caught a lion
Escaping in the foam.
The crowds edged cautiously back to the quay
And so our convoy with its lions set out
For Rome and arenas foul with blood.

At night we sleep in snatches.
In lulls a sudden roar will go
From lion to lion and ship to ship.
They smell each other in the night-wind.
Anchored in a bay we heard
A lion's voice from the hills,
And the darkness resounded with every lion
Roaring for freedom and Africa.

We are dogged by fear and guilt on our voyage,
Imagining the death in the arena
Of these amiable friends
Who happily take raw meat we throw them.
Gently and casually a male
Lays his paw upon his female and looks about
Snarling at any threat to her.

Having mastered the lions, we find
The lions have mastered us.
Our clothes are musty from lion hair and dung,
And some nights we dance and sing songs by torchlight,
Watched by lions, their whiskers sensing the air.
Asleep we dream of cages for ourselves,
From which cooped up we stare at lions
Freely roaming on deck and sniffing the sea.

Noel Macainsh

Home

A pause, but never arrival
(progress passes through):
the heart of change is survival,
the house is fashioned anew—

31

O stationary Middle Ages:
Urbis et Orbis—Rome!
Just one of numerous stages:
heaven cooped in a dome.

Obscure, successive fathers
(some sixty sires since Christ)
fell in with various muses:
fertile ones sufficed,
charmed the yawning bowsprit
up over phase and phase,
from moribund tribe and village
through boundless, numinous haze.

Beacon-light at the masthead:
a pallid cerebral glow
flaring the winds of knowledge,
lusting to know and know;
folders, maps, procedures,
routes that never end—
though vistas flatter to failure,
re-group, re-trace, amend:

Pitched to the south of Asia,
build on a knobbled hill,
escape from a puritan father:
the same inherited will
fights to achieve the freehold—
wife, children, land—
build on a floating planet
a house that will not stand:

Here are the restless futures,
the dwarfish, impish brood
revived in a role that reaches
past all the past pursued:
by shelves of ill-used sages,
mock of Greece and Rome,
borne on the wash of ages,
they laugh—and call it home.

Peter Porter

A Hoplite's Helmet

Inside this metal
A brain known to great brains

Moved to kill,
The object was in the orders.

The helmetless lover
And boozer fathered as many

New skulls as any
But he put the helmet back on. You can

Frighten the cat
Poking your fingers through the eye pieces.

When death's eyes
Make a play for me let him approach

In this helmet;
It's sat on some howling scenes—

Witness the old lady
Of Corinth who couldn't be parted

From her sponges;
A yellow bean drying—that was a chunk

Of Epaminondas's brain,
You meet the greatest people in battle.

The helmet's worth
A hundred pounds. Verdigris takes

A month to form
And lasts two thousand years. As many

Million dead
Must come again before this metal dies.

John Rowland

At Noosa

All day the house blooms like a sail
    With air and light,
Trembles at anchor on its gaptoothed piles
In a seawind soft as talc, that touches and again touches
    Like a sweet mother. Spade and pail
Trip us by open doors, pennies and shells
Scatter on ledges and on windowsills

With combs, my thongs, your lipstick, safety-pins.
    Sand in the shower,
Salty towels on the veranda rail;
The worn mirror's bloodshot brown eye
    Shows us each evening darker skins,
Eyes clearer, bleaching hair. Sunstruck, we lie
At ease or swim or climb the rocks, or play

At sandcastles on the dazzling field
    Of empty beach
Plump as the children's faces, that grow warm
And smooth and simple to the touch as sand.
    At dark the children yield
Willingly to sleep, as the sea sound
Builds over the house a temple, round

Columns and low roof, that rise
    Close by our windows, where
The folding surf renews its hiss and crumple,
Vague white on white in darkness, till the moon
    Swelling towards fullness like the days
Restores the distance, floods the sky with milk,
The sea with diamond flashes, breathing silk

Scents in our faces. As we find each other
    A child laughs in sleep
And still we have uncounted days, our view
Ends in no cliff, the beach is ours,
    Morning fulfils the stars' pledge of fair weather.
All true; yet items in the full account
Are sandflies, washing-up, mosquitoes, rent,

Three days' rain, and something like a quarrel.
    Lara and Zhivago
Had no children, nor is laundry mentioned
By Lawrence in a similar situation

With Frieda in the cottage at Thirroul:
It makes a certain difference to the tone.
Exaltation needs to be alone

And art selects; but if we take the whole
    Seldom we shall
Do better, or be better as ourselves.
Be thankful, then, the mosquitoes were so few,
    The time so radiant that if we did fail
Our failures served to toughen the alloy,
As stars give sense to night, or night to day.

Thomas W. Shapcott

Water Skier

Water fans apart and gasps
beneath the skier's blade-swift skill
and even the river's wading reeds
gasp semaphores of praise at all

this rippling youth's display and ease.
Firm and tanned beneath day's curve
of sky the dexterous rider patterns
river-long his rapid love,

alive and flashing in the summer
reach; and all his triumph is
this moment's mastery of flesh.
And here his only conquest lies.

Spelling the symbols of his pride
in water's manuscript, he grooves
a trembling chapter with his skis
which, even as he laughs, dissolves.

R. A. Simpson

Science Fiction Story

A droplet down the sky
Grew to a metal sphere.

It landed and it waited
The emissaries of Earth.
Terror had not abated

And yet we sent our legions
To knock upon its door;
And each report told us
The creatures, though all green,
Were not imperious.

But those who spoke of them
Returned with milky eyes,
And soon we learnt the power
Of quick, mesmeric rays:
They have ruled us from that hour.

Vivian Smith

At an Exhibition of Historical Paintings, Hobart

The sadness in the human visage stares
out of these frames, out of these distant eyes;
the static bodies painted without love
that only lack of talent could disguise.

Those bland receding hills are too remote
where the quaint natives squat with awkward calm.
One carries a kangaroo like a worn toy;
his axe alert with emphasised alarm.

Those nearer woollen hills are now all streets;
even the water in the harbor's changed.
Much is alike and yet a slight precise
disparity seems intended and arranged—

as in that late pink terrace's facade.
How neat the houses look. How clean each brick.
One cannot say they look much older now,
but somehow more themselves, less accurate.

And see the pride in this expansive view:
churches, houses, farms, a prison tower:
a grand gesture like wide-open arms
showing the artist's trust, his clumsy power.

And this much later vision, grander still:
the main street sedate carriages unroll
towards the inappropriate, tentative mountain:
a flow of lines the artist can't control

the foreground nearly breaks out of its frame
the streets end so abruptly in the water. . . .
But how some themes return. A whaling ship.
The last natives. Here that silent slaughter

is really not prefigured nor avoided.
One merely sees a profile, a full face,
a body sitting stiffly in a chair:
the soon-forgotten absence of a race. . . .

Album pieces: bowls of brown glazed fruit . . .
I'm drawn back yet again to those few studies
of native women whose long floral dresses
made them first aware of their own bodies.

History has made artists of all these
painters without energy or feature.
But how some gazes cling. Around the hall
the pathos of the past, the human creature.

Randolph Stow

The Singing Bones

> *'Out where the dead men lie.'*—Barcroft Boake

Out there, beyond the boundary fence, beyond
the scrub-dark flat horizon that the crows
returned from, evenings, days of rusty wind
raised from the bones a stiff lament, whose sound
netted my childhood round, and even here still blows.

My country's heart is ash in the market-place,
is aftermath of martyrdom. Out there
its sand-enshrined lay saints lie piece by piece,
Leichardt by Gibson, stealing the wind's voice,
and Lawson's tramps, by choice made mummia and air.

No pilgrims leave, no holy-days are kept
for these who died of landscape. Who can find,
even, the campsites where the saints last slept?

37

Out there their place is, where the charts are gapped,
unreachable, unmapped, and mainly in the mind.

But Out from Noonkanbah and Back of Bourke
they streamed, it seems, like lemmings, in a surge.
For time meant tucker, tramp they must (for work,
or vision, or bravado) on—Outback—
to leave at last a pack, one boot, and dirge on dirge.

They were all poets, so the poets said,
who kept their end in mind in all they wrote
and hymned their bones, and joined them. Gordon died
happy, one surf-loud dawn, shot through the head,
and Boake astonished, dead, his stockwhip round his throat.

Time, time and time again, when the inland wind
beats over myall from the dunes, I hear
the singing bones, their glum Victorian strain.
A ritual manliness, embracing pain
to know; to taste terrain their heirs need not draw near.

Chris Wallace-Crabbe

Disturbance of a Scholar

One must admit that order holds full sway
On the baked surface of our colony,
Palm trees in line, facades in unison,
Roads running east and west
From a charmed sea to neat surburban hills;
And, I must say,
There is a kind of order visible
In these tall bookshelves, logically arranged
To range all knowledge alphabetically
Far from the scholarship of mildew.
This room of reason, where I teach and rule,
Looks mildly out on the climate's alternations—
That broiling, frying, stewing of the wits—
For cool is only rational, you know.

Some of my students carry the breath of rumour,
Hinting the native quarter smells rebellion.
I couldn't be sure at all;
But the Governor's a heat-besotted fool
Who, from his whisky-blur,

Sees politics in terms of God and evil.
He'll drag the mountains down upon his head.
But that is mere surmise. My pupils grow
More numerous every term and know
The ways of democratic compromise.
One must admit that order holds full sway,
Spreading like irrigation through the land,
Drawn from this college
Which taps the springs of order visibly;
Our minds are fresh, our faculties quite calm.

And yet, and yet, however damp winds rattle
Through these uncertain dated palms,
However nature breathes upon the earth,
This itch of lust I had not reckoned with . . .
What if my students nodding over books
Here and there in this lucid library
Are seen as women, nodding in full flower?
What if Flaubert and Tolstoy only fan
Deep flames with which they naturally burn?
(For I burn too, and bloom.)
What if I touch one hand
And feel it tremble sympathetically?
What if I smile too easily in response?
Am I responsible?
And where does reason triumph in all this?
Satan, I smiled and said that you were dead,
Killed before 1900, killed by books
And by the mind's unerring flight of darts.
Perhaps you are,
Perhaps you are indeed,
Dead as the broken gods museums hold.

And yet, and yet, what other force would move me,
Driven to refuge in a library
That is no haven but a still hothouse
Heavy with flowers and fruit?
Alas, the wind-lashed palms are far more stable
Swaying in file along the esplanades;
But I seem blown by strange disordered winds:
I don't know where they're blowing from, or to.

Chris Wallace-Crabbe

Going to Sleep

Now switchfall darkness drenches all the room;
Entanglements of line and form are swept
Out of your ken; well-fingered shapes become
The one broad shape of night
And who can tell what sullen rules are kept?

Out there, beyond the cot-bars, what remains?
Wallpaper, rough towels, wooden toys,
Forbidden cupboards and a shattered train—
All these are sunken deep;
No vase can fall, no being makes a noise.

The bars that you can feel enclose a world,
The circumscribed dominion of King Touch.
As blind as Oedipus and strangely cold
You grip your blanket, hear
Far trams, a muffled radio: not much.

A father and a mother drift away.
Tossed on the flux, their independent boats
Eddy and swirl beyond Port Phillip Bay,
Enter the open sea;
Cupped in the blue god's hand their marriage floats.

Withdraw into your blanket. Shut your eyes.
Feckless imagination flirts with death
And must be drowned. Relax and realize
That sun will lick your panes
And white clouds blossom on your morning breath.

Griffith Watkins

The Black Cockatoos

Weather changes all predicaments.
When the first rains
drip and tamper with the barometer's
itchy finger, the ground spelling out
neat, odorous secrets,

the black cockatoos struggle
and blunder
south.
    They come
sawing round the edge of Melon hill,
whooping and spilling epithets
that breakfast coffee makes oblique.
    They shudder and make jagged
motifs on the clean air as rollicky tails
flash flints of red.
They fly south then, croaking and laughing.

When the mind slackens its perimeters
the winds move in.
Some of us, who are trying too hard not
to be clever, find that our hearts are
being sucked dry by junk in newspapers,
books and television.
But the cockatoos remind us of the healing
universe outdoors.
They screech hilarity and squash the groggy
air with scraggy wings and fly south
for seed.

What is never available is the state,
condition, suppleness of mind,
                    body,
                     soul.
No gauges tell us how we stand.

We fall among thieves, act lunatic,
improvident, are blasphemous, give
short shrift to those who love us best,
grumble and let our image
slip.
But the cockatoos, black as sin, hoary
and uncontrite, give hints of what we
need, which is what they need too, i.e.—
the landscape's sun, wind, sea and rain.
We need to get out from under our roofs.
Out from inside our cars.
We need to let sun, sea, wind and rain
sluice over us.
We need to steal some of the dignity
of trees, rocks and ourselves grow above
the placating earth.

For the evils we accumulate can best
be dispelled by the very elements
the black cockatoos praise best.

Milton Acorn

Honesty

Honesty is the blood
of the mind,
as money is the blood
of this damned society.

No, I've made it
too personal, it's
a love affair
with all human things
that enter me;

with myself really,
for I incarnate
a multitude of voices
and works
of love and anger,

with or without
my will
tho the will helps.

Take care you
confirm yourself
with deeds,
lest when you peel
the last onion-skin
from your soul
you find nothing.

Margaret Atwood

The City Planners

Cruising these residential Sunday
streets in dry August sunlight:
what offends us is
the sanities;
the houses in pedantic rows, the planted
sanitary trees, assert
levelness of surface like a rebuke
to the dent in our car door.

No shouting here, or
shatter of glass; nothing more abrupt
than the rational whine of a power mower
cutting a straight swath in the discouraged grass.

But though the driveways neatly
sidestep hysteria
by being even, the roofs all display
the same slant of avoidance to the hot sky,
certain things:
the smell of spilled oil a faint
sickness lingering in the garages,
a splash of paint on brick surprising as a bruise,
a plastic hose poised in a vicious
coil; even the too-fixed stare of the wide windows

give momentary access to
the landscape behind or under
the future cracks in the plaster

when the houses, capsized, will slide
obliquely into the clay seas, gradual as glaciers
that right now nobody notices.

That is where the City Planners
with the insane faces of political conspiritors
are scattered over unsurveyed
territories, concealed from each other:
each in his own private blizzard;

guessing directions, they sketch
transitory lines rigid as wooden borders
on a wall in the white vanishing air
tracing the panic of suburb
order in a bland madness of snows.

Margaret Atwood

Descents

Grandfather on his apple farms
had fear of rabbits
for the saplings, and would track them down
at snowfall with gun and snare,
string them across his winters
(their dead blood apple-red and
civilized to pies).

43

Now my father
among his brambly acres
lets the snake sun where
it wants to but wars
on groundhogs, skunks, digs
kneedeep fences filled with glass
and wire around his lettuces;
but with their noses nibbling
the scent of cauli-
flower, woodchucks out-
fox him; beaver dams unlock
his meadows to the swamp and weeds
encroach across his fences
(and he shoots, moves rocks, cuts
roots, fires to protect
this planned and planted growing).

So
in me stalk
with their apple trees and axes
and upright hardhanded
love of straight lines and corners
generations of men
winning their sanity in one long
wrestle with the forest,
asserting: Here will be gardens.

I have given
up that fight (or have I?),
say when waking
let the wil-
derness tangle where it will
somewhere out there;
after all
that, this
is now a city surely.

But in sleeping there are still
moments when the brain's leaves
rustle
        (here will be gardens)
and I stand beside my tumbled fences
watching as the rodent
eyes, the unpredicted claws
draw near, not certain
whether I should
smile or kill.

Luella Booth

The Most I Know of Courage

The most I know of courage, I learned
from my Irish mother, who died loudly
shortly after flirting
with one of the hospital clergy.

Who cut huge bouquets
of blue larkspur and orange lilies
every 12th of July, winking,
'to hell with the Pope.'

Who fell from riches to rags and rose
into world's estate,
fighting my father's virus-ridden brain
for its castrated brilliancy, and wept
for the first time in my hearing
when he died finally
of pneumonia.

Who sat with my sister and I
summer evenings
breathing the rich hot scent
of ferny smallplants, geraniums
in clay pots, suspending
the roofedge of the battered porch,
saying, and I quote,

'It's all out there children and waiting
the pain and the ecstacy
the fire and the water. Can you
hear it moving, smell it, taste it?
Can you touch it, *feel* it?—it's there
ripe for your taking, when you're ready
after the growing and groping,
the building inside
of the spirit to house it.'

Children it's there waiting . . .

George Bowering

Moon Shadow

Last night the rainbow
round the moon

climbed with how sad steps
as I walked home

colour surrounding me,
cloud around my head.

    I am moon!
    Arrows fly at me!

    I slide cold and pale
    over cold earth
    of Alberta winter!

    I show one face
    to the world,
    immaculate still,
    inscrutable female
    male animal ball
    of rock
    shining with borrowed light

      rolling in that light
      the other side of
      forgetful space!

I am a shining tear
of the sun

full moon, silver,
who but myself knows
where the sun shall set?

I am able to instruct
the whole universe,

instruct the heart,
the weeping eye,
of any single man.

Slide over the moon-
lit earth, a shadow
of a chariot.

Walk homeward
forgetful where I have been

with how sad steps
my shadow before me

on the earth, moon shadow
rainbow round my heart,
wondering where in the universe I am.

Leonard Cohen

On Hearing a Name Long Unspoken

Listen to the stories
men tell of last year
that sound of other places
though they happened here

Listen to a name
so private it can burn
hear it said aloud
and learn and learn

History is a needle
for putting men asleep
anointed with the poison
of all they want to keep

Now a name that saved you
has a foreign taste
claims a foreign body
froze in last year's waste

And what is living lingers
while monuments are built
then yields its final whisper
to letters raised in gilt

But cries of stifled ripeness
whip me to my knees
I am with the falling snow
falling in the seas

I am with the hunters
hungry and shrewd
and I am with the hunted
quick and soft and nude

I am with the houses
that wash away in rain
and leave no teeth of pillars
to rake them up again

Let men numb names
scratch winds that blow
listen to the stories
but what you know you know

And knowing is enough
for mountains such as these
where nothing long remains
houses walls or trees

John Robert Colombo

John Bunyan in the Midnight Hold

Caught up in an epidemic of enthusiasm,
the tinker saved his poor countrymen—
for the second, third and fourth times.

'But the folk were already converted
in that part of England.'

The parish bells at Bedfordshire
developed palsy, clanged incessantly,
when he as much as neared the neighbourhood.

'Some say he himself
rang the Bedfordshire bells.'

In scandalous squalor, pomp of war,
a Living Concordance of the Book,
wisdom was scribbled across his pages.

'The syntax was subject
to the corrector of the press.'

From his twelve-year prison he roared:
'I envy the very stones of the streets,
and the very tiles of the houses!'

And worried: 'The wind must not blow
on my blind daughter.'

Faithful enemy, false friend,
dear companion, dull brethren—
not one complained of his craftsmanship.

'When he tinkered with the kettles,
they *stayed* fixed!'

John Robert Colombo

Riverdale Lion

Bound lion, almost blind from meeting their gaze and popcorn,
the Saturday kids love you. It is their parents
who would paint your mane with polkadots to match their
　　　California shirts
and would trim your nails for tieslips.

Your few roars delight them. But they wish you would quicken
　　　your pace
and not disappear so often into your artificial cave
for there they think you partake of secret joys and race
through the jungle-green lair of memory
under an African sun as gold as your mane.

But you fool them. You merely suffer the heat and scatter the
　　　flies
with your tail. You never saw Africa.
The sign does not tell them that you were born here, in captivity,
that you are as much a Canadian as they are.

Deborah Eibel

Kayak Sickness

The hours are curvatures, the days are rings
Concentric with the hunter of the seal:

49

Within the bounds of circles, he aligns
Himself with mysteries that facts conceal.

A storm is promising on August seas:
The kayak overturns; the hunter drifts
Within it, under time, locating seals;
The boat turns upright, and he claims these gifts.

Sea rage is blessed friction in the north:
It keeps a man awake to his harpoon,
Awake to nothing else. He does not see
That sun and kayak intersect at noon.

But this is all he sees in time of calm:
On sleeping waters light obscures a map
Of mysteries so readable in storms,
And kayak embarkation is a trap.

Hypnosis is the work of light and time:
The hunter ebbs away into a cell
Within himself, away from magic seals,
Until a wind can break the hateful spell.

Joan Finnigan

Noon Hour

Noon-hour

and the children come in
like wind
wild at the door,
blowing the stale
and dusty world

they charge me,
the morning at school
pitched like a javelin
into the cave.

'Look, mummy!
We had Civil Defence today!
They showed us how to do this—

Isn't it funny?'

And they go into Arab positions
of prayer on the floor,
the little snow-flakes
of their hands,
clasped tight behind their heads,
elbows tucked in about their ears,
bottoms in the air.

'You should get near a wall.'

'This is to protect the jugular veins.'

They give a giggling good
description
of flying glass
fashioned into daggers

And my little one comes in
from the end of her record,
'Here we go round the mulberry bush',
quickly joins her brothers
in their game,
curling into a little laughing
doom-ball on the floor.

(Yes, I suppose that is as idiotic
a position as any—
putting one's back to it
and shutting one's eyes;
make it acceptable
by pretending there is
a defence—)

Oh, never was Woman so cold and small
in the steam-kettle mists
of the children
gone back to school

But I must do more than wring
my hands.

George Johnston

The Bargain Sale

The time has come, I'm going to sell
My photograph of the abyss
Which I've had framed to look like hell,
An *objet d'art* I won't much miss:
I have some other things as well
More or less obsolete like this,
Some have been treasures, some have not,
I'm putting prices on the lot.

Here is a thing a sage might wear
For queasy stomach, clammy palm,
Other forebodings of despair:
This is my mask of Stoic calm.
Ageing but still in good repair
It's covered me from qualm to qualm
But I've grown big or it's grown small,
Now it won't fit my case at all.

Under my handkerchiefs and scent
While I was rummaging one day
Look what I found: the sentiment
Embrace your Fate, like new, slight fray.
Here is an antique ornament
Some weltanshauung might well display.
A favourite item once upon
A time. Ah well, the sale is on.

Why do I want to sell my stuff
In these exciting days? I know
That life is earnest, time is tough,
But me, I'm not, I'm soft and slow.
Look, I'm not asking half enough,
My prices are absurdly low,
Bargains out of this world are they:
Hurry, before they fade away.

Gwendolyn MacEwen

Appendectomy

It's interesting how you can brag about a scar;
I'm fascinated with mine, it is diagonal and straight,
it suggests great skill, great speed,
it is no longer or shorter than it needs to be.

It is good how it follows my natural symmetry
parallel to the hip, a perfect geometry;
it is not a wound; it is a diagram
drawn correctly; it has no connection with pain.

It's interesting how you can brag about a scar;
nothing in nature is a straight line
except this delightful blasphemy on my belly;
the surgeon was an Indian, and beautiful, and holy.

Jay MacPherson

The Beauty of Job's Daughters

The old, the mad, the blind have fairest daughters.
Take Job; the beasts the accuser sends at evening
Shoulder his house and shake it; he's not there,
Attained in age to inwardness of daughters,
In all the land no women found so fair.

Angels and sons of God are nearest neighbours,
And even the accuser may repair
To walk with Job in pleasures of his daughters,
Wide shining rooms more warmly lit at evening,
Gardens beyond whose secrets scent the air.

Not wiles of men nor envy of the neighbours.
Riches of earth, nor what heaven holds more rare,
Can take from Job the beauty of his daughters,
The gardens in the rock, music at evening,
And cup so full that all who come must share.

Perhaps we passed them? It was late, or evening,
And surely those were desert stumps, not daughters,

In fact we doubt that they were ever there.
The old, the mad, the blind have fairest daughters.
In all the land no women found so fair.

Tom Marshall

Niagara

You the beginning
of all
my stormy journey
closer
and closer to terror.

For truth is also terror.
In the riding wind
stand
like disintegrating oracles
the widening rounds
of your roses.

To survive
I would want
to see you
with the cold
detachment of a god.

I know
it is
because of you
intolerant of weakness
I go

my heart-sick
bold
broken-tongued way
to wisdom
and the doubtful rectitude
of controllable despair.

Rona Murray

Charm

Lift your cup and find me stretched
Between the water and your lip;
The thirsting never shall be quenched
By water from a blue-edged cup.

Stand, outcast man, before the fire,
Find my shadow huge between
Warmth and your pale shrinking skin:
No fire may straight the crooked bone.

Run across the crumbled world,
Hide within the creviced rock,
Still your mind confronts my mind
In the mirror of the dark.

When the winter winds have stripped
Each aching ounce of tawdry flesh,
When the proud chameleon heart
Has died of its own curled deceit,
Then at last you may escape
Perilous love and perilous hate.

John Newlove

The Dog

Lying on my back
on the hot prairie
dreaming of
the nervous sea,

my ·22 rifle
by my side, my dog
ranging about and snuffing,
content that I

should do nothing, for
he was a damn fool
of a dog, red and curly,
and always scared

away the crows or gophers
before I could shoot,
dreaming of the sea
and anything to do except

what was at hand
I spent the summers,
never thinking anyone
would love me,

never caring beyond
the delight at making
myself feel sad
and the false tears

tightening my throat
as I worked myself down,
never thinking anyone
could love me, not

as I love myself—except
that red dog, damn fool
running and barking
away toward the town.

Alden Nowlan

The Migrant Hand

For how many thousands of years, for how many millions
of baskets and wagonloads and truckloads of onions,
or cotton, or turnips has this old man knelt
in the dirt of sun-crazy fields? If you ask him,
he'll put you off: he's suspicious of questions.
The truth is that Adam, a day out of Eden,
started him gathering grapes: old Pharoah
sold him to Greece; he picked leeks for the Seljuks,
garlic for Tuscans, Goths and Normans,
pumpkins and maize for the Pilgrim Fathers,
has forgotten them all, forgotten all of the past, except
the last ten hours of blackflies and heat,
the last two hundred barrels of potatoes.

David Wevill

The Space Flier

And now he is dressed, snugly and with care,
Buttoned, muffled and padded as by
His mother's hands, to face the snow outdoors.

He strides into a dazzling light like snow,
Arc-lights that blot his shadow, the rustle of faces
Peering, applauding, make a gauntlet of his path

Shimmering to the steel rungs. The man is calm as he climbs.
The crowd quietens, admiring their uncertainty,
And no one rubs his charmed eyes to reflect

How gradually a man, groping, achieves himself,
Painfully, as the touch of his life infects,
Poisons at his fingertips the burst stone and the burnt

Cherry-tree, the millions dead, greater than numbers of stars;
And the risk that stutters in the winking eyes
Of his steel crib, past breath of straw and

Cattle in Christ's manger. And now,
If nothing blunders, his life will flower
Too suddenly, like a tulip with false heat,

A botanist's trick, to catch the applause
Of wits and innocents, to throw ambition
Reliefed against the sky where he is the hunter

Jacklighting with the slow hook of his flight
The risky shapes that break
His night's surface like corks, subside with a splash

And vanish. But his dangers, they say
Are charted, planned with care; it is their hearts,
The watchers, that leap

Far higher than he can go, down into the profound
Uncertainty of their skulls swollen to take
No new knowledge, but to confirm old fears,

The reticence of a lame man, of a snowballing boy
Whose fingers freeze against the injuring chance
To act. And none pity him—

It is themselves they pity. The fires
That could lick him up are tongues they'd praise him with,
Like scolding mothers, scorning their failure, a man

Whose nature, betraying their effort, would steal
Quick grief by his downfall, and be memorialized,
His cinder to stone. But now none pity him—

'See, this is a tough one!' the watchers shout,
'His arching snowball will not melt in his hands,'
And watch the fire of his trajectory scorching higher

Beyond tangent and compass of their suffering.

Edward Brathwaite

Jou'vert

I

He was a slave
To drums, to flutes, brave

Brass and rhythm. The jump-up saved
Him from the thought of holes, damp,

Rain through the roof of his have-
Nothing cottage. Kele, Kalinda-stamp,

The limbo, calypso-season camp:
These he loved best of all: the road-march tramp

Down Princess Street, round Mar-
Evale: Kitch, Sparrow, Dougla, these were the stars

Of his melodic heaven. Their little winking songs car-
Ried him back to days of green unhur-

Ried growing. The Car-
Nival's apotheosis blazed for two nights

Without fear or sorrow, colour bar
Or anyone to question or restrain his height-

Ened, borrowed glory. He walked so far
On stilts of songs, of masqueraded story. Stars

Were near. Doors of St. Peter's heaven were ajar.
Mary, Christ's Christmas mother was there

Too, her sweet inclined compassion
In full view. In such bright swinging company

He could no longer feel the cramp
Of poverty's confinement, spirit's damp.

He could have all he wished, he ever
Wanted. But the good stilts splinter-

Ed, wood legs broke, calypso steel pan
Rhythm faltered. The midnight church

Bell fell across the glow, the lurch-
Ing cardboard crosses. Behind the masks, grave

Lenten sorrows waited: Ash-
Wednesday, ashes, darkness, graves.

After the bambalula bambulai
He was a slave again.

II

But

Bambalula Bambulai
Bambalula Bambulai

Stretch the drum
Tight hips will sway

Stretch the back
Tight whips will flay

Bambalula Bambulai
Bambalula Bambulai

Kink the gong gong
Swoop and sway

Ashes come
And Christ will pray

Christ will pray
To Odomankoma

Nyame God
And Nyankopon

And

Bambalula Bambulai
Bambalula Bambulai

Dust of desert
Cries of arrows

Boulders roll
And coils of shadows

Boulders roll
And rivers thunder

Lightning flashes
Man assunder

Bambalula Bambulai
Bambalula Bambulai

Fangs of lightning
Strike and

Bite the bitter
World of stone

And sorrows

Bambalula Bambulai
Bambalula Bambulai

But the sorrows
Burn to ashes

Grey rocks
Melt to pools

Of lashes'
Sweat and flowers

Bloom along the way

Bambalula Bambulai
Bambalula Bambulai

Flowers bloom
Their tom tom

Lashes raising
Little steel pan

Petals to the music's
Doom

As the ping pong
Dawn comes

Riding
Over shattered homes

61

And furrows
Over fields

And musty ghettos
Over men now

Hearing
Waiting

Watching
In the Lent-

En morning
Hurts for-

Gotten, hearts
No longer bound

To black and bitter
Ashes in the ground

Now waking
Making

Making
With their

Rhythms some-
Thing torn

And new.

Note: Two days before the beginning of Lent, the people of Trinidad—like people in most Catholic countries—have a Carnival: two days of colourful costumed dance ('jump-up'), when most people forget themselves, their fears and their worries in the wonder and rhythm of the occasion. What makes the Trinidad Carnival unique is the use, as an integral part of the festivities, of the Steel Band—a fantastic collection of musical pots and pans that can play anything from Bartok to calypso. These 'pans', made mostly from oil drums, are carved on their playing surfaces into octave facets which resemble the petals of the hibiscus flower—hence 'little steel pan petals' in the poem. The smaller, treble-toned pans are called 'ping pongs', but it is the big bass drums that move the 'road marches' along and give impetus to the whole proceeding. *Bambalula Bambulai* is a rendition of this rhythm which begins at dawn: Jou'vert (Jour Ouvert): on the first day of Carnival and continues on until the midnight that marks the solemn beginning of the Christian Lent.

Frank Collymore

Schooner

By the dip of the sky, runaway water under the stars,
The ship's prow drips from the lash of the wave, and
The sails' saga is told in slow syllables as we plunge onward
Towards the shore of the horizon where the clouds are wrapped
About a shadow.   The helmsman's face, old as stone,
Is etched upon the darkness by the cigarette's glow, his cap
Pulled low about his ears. Voyaging is slow
And mists spiral through the waiting mind; the night is long,
And the sails' song interminable; moments glide
From darkness into darkness. Fugue of forgetting,
While stars rush silently in swooping curves, and the night
Is hooped around the sea's endlessness. The cigarette stub
Shrinks into nothingness, the hub of thought recedes,
And tattered shreds are scattered upon the silent deck
Lost among unfamiliar shadows. Wan as forgotten dawns
The lantern in the binnacle. Where the huddled hatch
Catches the threading light, thought's snails leave slimy tracks
As meaningless as the word-cipher of a dream. There is
No meaning here but the song of the sails, no end
To wandering. And across the waters strides the wind
To lay its reckless head upon the bosom of the night.

Karl Sealy

On the Emmaus Road

*An extract from 'He is Risen', an Easter poem for voices.
Cleophas speaks.*

I was not keen on Emmaus that day;
My thoughts made angle at Jerusalem
The hub and centre of his circling acts:
There would I fain have moped, wallowing listlessly
In sorrow's tideless pool, whose brackish waters filch
Desire for food, weakening you for the tug
Of their strong undercurrents. But Simeon
Although he too was dazed and sorrowful
At the grim climax of the swift events,

Woodpeckered me about some urgent skins
We were working on; moreover, he declared,
The seven-mile walk to Emmaus would do
Both of us good, for there is nothing like,
You know, a good long trek to dissipate
Melancholy, and doctor psychic ills.
So I gave way. But we'd not gone a mile
When we, as often happens to a traveller,
Found rumour had outstripped us:
For as we passed a field where women worked
We heard words tossed concerning Christ's tomb,
How it'd been found empty, how the stone was moved,
The absence of death's smell, how the broached vault
Had been perfumed by angels, even how
He had appeared in flesh and blood to some.
We halted and da capoed this loud news,
Sounding it over as a harpist sounds
His brain's creation, critical of its ring,
Wary of false notes in its lyric truth.
I was for our immediate return
Unto Jerusalem to find how true
Or otherwise might be these women's words:
But Simeon pressed for no, reminding me
Of our given word to have some skins
Ready upon a certain day; then he said
That I might return to Jerusalem
And find the truth out; however he'd go on
To Emmaus, and working hard alone
Still meet our obligation, if he could.
We had agreed on this, and I'd promised him
To join him ere the day was shadowless
When he set off; but as I watched him go,
I remembered how he had not been well
Not long before. The odds were on
That if I let him go he'd overtax
His just returning strength, and take too much
Perhaps of sun: therefore I curbed awhile
My eagerness for the truth, and clapping after him,
Joined him again, telling him I'd send
One of my sister's sons to Peter's house
To make inquiry. As we trudged on
We swapped experiences of His acts
That we had actually seen, and matched His words
With those of others who had gone before.

About halfway to Emmaus is a track
Between two fields. As we approached this spot,

We saw a tall man stroll from this green lane
And fall in step beside us. Simeon there
Was nearer to him, so I left it to him
To grunt a greeting: for I must confess
That we both have an innate distrust of
Too friendly strangers; next the stranger said
That if a subject of discussion held
Two so engaged, there certainly was, he'd think,
Room for a third. I answered him that if
He did not know the traitorous events of
The last few days within Jerusalem
He walked alone. It pleased him to assume
Ignorance still; so I related from
Judas' kiss at Thursday's furry dusk,
The mockeries of trials, the people's glee
At Jesus' bloody side, and finally
The story that the weeding women told.
That was his cue. Never again shall I,
Plodding the dusty roads of Judaea,
Walk within touch of such an expounder
Of holy things. Reason and lucid speech
Were fused for us for nearly half the way
To Emmaus; and always, as he spoke,
The stranger turned his face towards the hedge
Whenever either Simeon or I
Tried to improve upon our knowledge of
His features' profile. When we reached our home
He bade farewell and made as he'd go on
Through the village; but we both begged him to—
As he squatted down and sketched leaves in the dust—
Tarry with us and have a snack at least.
After some time he did agree and I
Busied myself with some dried fish we had
Whilst Simeon made some cakes of barley flour.
At last we sat down to our table of
Roughly hewn wood. He blessed the food, and then
Those large, strong hands reached for the steaming bread,
And pliant fingers broke a loaf in two.
Our mouths gaped wide; not to receive the food
That he gave us, but with the wonder of
Recognition; for we were two of those
Numbering five thousand whom he satisfied
With what would hardly fill one fisherman.

O. R. Dathorne

Letter from Lagos

In your mourning for sun
On your dull winter morning,
I wish you life and light
And joy, when your red winter sun
Cuts itself out of the dull cardboard sky.

Here on a clear independent morning,
The white sun kow-tows to the blue wave at Bar-beach.
And children curve thirsty feet
Like shingle
To the archetypal mould of incoming sea.

On the wharf the greedy fingers of cranes
Dig deep into the hole of a ship's hold.

For the federal sun
To imprisoned here,
Can only telegraph his greetings
Over the paper sky.

Slade Hopkinson

Worthing: Midnight

Arrest the clockwork of the world,
Place a rough palm on the sky,
Now that in every wood
Of the fanned, coral-twigged sea,
In the folds of every furled
Cloth of weeds where shy fish stood
Today in salt-strained light,
In the grooved symmetry
Of the waves' footprints on their floor,
And in the pools that lie
For high tide through the reef's door,
In the unwinking sight
Of the moon on its eucharist height,
Beneath the whipping wind
66 And the stars hung in chains,

In each sea-chamber, on each kind
Sofa or coverlet weed
Every lithe flank, every shell,
Each finned or prickled breed
Wears the camouflage of sleep
And quietly disdains
The possibly waking net
Or curious teeth from the deep.
Now the sky's dial tells
Midnight; while on the shore
The crabs in red and jet
Cool in their nests of sand
Have tucked in legs and eyes,
And each long-necked bird in a core
Of plumage has hidden its head.

It is some hours too late
For any sound of fisherman's wand
Or bargaining by the boat
After the toil of the net
From sun low to sun straight
To dew-time of the sun's bed
And the chill locked out with a coat;
Some hours beyond the time
Of wives on the beach, and girls
With skirts full of shells,
Some hours beyond the time
Of the faces of my company.

      Yet,
Although the cunning mime
Of branches, as the wind curls
Its whip round sea-grape stems,
And the shadows' gaunt comedy
Play to only my eye,
Though drunks, fishermen's girls,
Voices, all my friends
Have gone, both tatters and pearls,
There is a pain which quells
That other—my intricate need,
And the coming hymn that I fear
And make without company.
At this hour and anvil I work,
Alone, to the wavelets' beat,
To break facility, greed,
Dishonesty's politeness, hate,

All the sins that lurk
In the sly nooks of the heart,
Approaching, I trust, the feat
Of ultimate innocence
And knowledge.
                    Now I celebrate
In my hymning fool's career
The careful singer's part
For my need's recompense.

A. J. Seymour

Morning in the Rupununi

Breathing the bracing air
The Lethem road curves round to Wichibai
And skirts the promontory Kanakus,
That sleep their ancient sleep.

Nothing has changed since the crazed driven men
From the recurrent drowned savannah
Dreamt El Dorado into myth
Shaped by that brave Elizabethan pen
And put insidious hope into Guiana's name
As a Fifth Columnist in history.

Impatient quick reward
Singing like siren from the soil
Not patiently extracted with the plough
In dovelike tilling—the gold, the diamond
That breaks the man to make a fortune
These flat slow-cropping lands grow a hardy cattle
Driving through gorges in a Wild West tale
That hangs the dust from hooves high in the air
The quiet Macushi like a mobile crop
Inherit still the patience of the soil.

A. J. Seymour
Blind Man's Buff

Whether he comes in hemlock
    as he came
    to Socrates,
Or quiet-faced
    in the evening
    with the soft-foot fall of dew,
or on a bullet
    humming, whining
    singing an iron greeting,
death will come to you.

It will not matter if
    you're a king with magnificent trappings,
    or a tramp through the starlight,
        out-at-knees, bearded,
        camel-like under his pack,

for reaching out
    impartial hands
the blind old gatherer
    will
    some day
    find you where you stand
    and take you back.

Edward Baugh

The Dictator has been Executed, Twentieth century Style

Perhaps,
when all is said,
that time was best
(no matter if my history is myth)
when barbarism raged in royal gold
and heads of rulers rolled
with leisured pomp and speeches.

Instead,
a lump of khaki-drill and boots
crumpled around unceremonious lead:
a flashbulb scoop, bandied about by screens,
nor left, one last and famous word
for benefit of keen anthologist.

Neville Dawes

Fugue

Have seen the summer convex of the wounded sky
want to catch it and clutch it and make it sing
of the wild wind's whisper and the hard-boiled sun
and the blue day kissing my mountain away
where the hawks dip wing-tipped diving.

Have seen the curved mane of the wind-whipped cane
want to snap it and squeeze it and make it rain
on the roots of the summer-tree withering
where my mountain mouths lie sleeping
and the hawks dip wing-tipped diving.

Have seen the curving prism of the rainbow's shaft
want to pluck it and plait it and make it bend
to pattern in the brain of the mountain top
where my grief is sighing like a fingered stop
where the hawks dip wing-tipped diving
and the graves are green at the world's end.

A. L. Hendriks

An Old Jamaican Woman thinks about the Hereafter

What would I do forever in a big place, who
have lived all my life in a small island?
The same parish holds the cottage I was born in, all
my family, and the cool churchyard.
                                    I have looked
up at the stars from my front verandah and have been afraid
of their pathless distances. I have never flown
in the loud aircraft nor have I seen palaces,
so I would prefer not to be taken up high nor
rewarded with a large mansion.
                                    I would like
to remain half-drowsing through an evening light
watching bamboo trees sway and ruffle for a valley-wind,
to remember old times but not to live them again;
occasionally to have a good meal with no milk
nor honey for I don't like them, and now and then to walk
by the grey sea-beach with two old dogs and watch
men bring up their boats from the water.
                                    For all this,
for my hope of heaven, I am willing to forgive my debtors
and to love my neighbour . . .
                                    although the wretch throws stones
at my white rooster and makes too much noise in her damn
      backyard.

A. L. Hendriks

Challenge

Had they been content with the obvious,
choosing the known belief,
voyaging not beyond sheltered harbours
or the habitual perimeter of charted ways;

had they been unwilling
to point from accustomed shores
and enter a strange horizon,

had they reefed sail
and beat homeward when the seas mountained
beyond Genoa;

had courage failed. . . .

Had they been content with theories
    (following Ptolemy),
querying not familiar skies
nor contesting the observed path of the daily sun;

had they preferred sleep and the dreams of night
to the cold intrigue of stars
moving strictly
above Pisa:

had thought been trapped. . . .

Had they been content with priestcraft,
performed the required rite,
challenging not dogma and authority of robes;

had they forgotten Lazarus
or sworn him a dark, unique phenomenon
when lean and angered beasts
circled
the Rome arena. . . .

Had they been content with the obvious
this age could appal us.

Evan Jones

The Song of the Banana Man

Touris', white man, wipin' his face,
Met me in Golden Grove market place.
He looked at m' ol' clothes brown wid stain,
An' soaked right through wid de Portlan' rain,
He cas' his eye, turn' up his nose,
He says, 'You're a beggar man, I suppose?'
He says, 'Boy, get some occupation,
Be of some value to your nation.'

I said, 'By God and dis big right han'
You mus' recognize a banana man.

'Up in de hills where de streams are cool,
An' mullet an' janga swim in de pool,
I have ten acres of mountain side,
An' a dainty-foot donkey dat I ride,
Four Gros Michel, an' four Lacatan,
Some coconut trees, an' some hills of yam,
An' I pasture on dat very same lan'
Five she-goats an' a big black ram,

'Dat, by God an' dis big right han'
Is de property of a banana man.

'I leave m'yard early-mornin' time
An' set m' foot to de mountain climb,
I ben' m' back to de hot-sun toil,
An' m' cutlass rings on de stony soil,
Ploughin' an' weedin', diggin' an' plantin'
Till Massa Sun drop back o' John Crow mountain,
Den home again in cool evenin' time,
Perhaps whistlin' dis likkle rhyme,

(SUNG) 'Praise God an' m' big right han'
I will live and die a banana man.

'Banana day is my special day,
I cut my stems an' I'm on m' way,
Load up de donkey, leave de lan'
Head down de hill to banana stan'.
When de truck comes roun', I take a ride
All de way down to de harbour side—
Dat is de night, when you, touris' man,
Would change your place wid a banana man.

'Yes, by God, an' m' big right han'
I will live and die a banana man.

'De bay is calm, an' de moon is bright,
De hills look black though the sky is light,
Down at de dock is an English ship,
Restin' after her ocean trip,
While on de pier is a monstrous hustle,
Tallymen, carriers, all in a bustle,
Wid stems on deir heads in a long black snake
Some singing de songs dat banana men make

73

'Like, (SUNG) 'Praise God an' m' big right han'
I will live an' die a banana man.

'Den de payment comes, an' we have some fun,
Me, Zekiel, Breda an' Duppy Son.
Down at de bar near United Wharf
We knock back a white rum, burs' a laugh,
Fill de empty bag for further toil
Wid saltfish, breadfruit, coconut oil.
Den head back home to m' yard to sleep,
A proper sleep dat is long an' deep.

'Yes, by God an' m' big right han'
I will live an' die a banana man.

'So when you see dese ol' clothes brown wid stain,
An' soaked right through wid de Portlan' rain,
Don't cas' your eye, nor turn your nose,
Don't judge a man by his patchy clothes,
I'm a strong man, a proud man, an' I'm free,
Free as dese mountains, free as dis sea,
I know myself, an' I know m' ways
An' will sing wid pride till de end o' m' days,

(SUNG) 'Praise God an' m' big right han'
I will live an' die a banana man.'

Cliff Lashley

Late November London

Late November London
and the trembling trees
raise their snarled arms in horror
to the leafless sky;
I walk
through autumn leaves
remembering the song
able to capture the feeling
though my eyes give the lie to the leaves,
mere litter.
Winter is coming on;
I long for my green green island
of the burnishing sun
where winter is hardly a word
and summer is all the seasons.

Edward Lucie-Smith

A Caged Beast

This other world: we cannot look at it
Without a lie—the looking is a lie.
'Like us,' we say, to all their calmer motions;
'Like us,' to every evidence of wit.
The narrow pupil of the leopard's eye
Contains more flattery than we'll admit;
We gesture there, performing our devotions
Not to the supple back, the rapid paw,
But to ourselves. That little mirror is
All of the leopard we have patience for.

But why so eager to catch likenesses?
The caged beast thrusts his head against the bars:
Two unreflecting wounds, two gazing scars.

Basil McFarlane

Ernest Hemingway, d. 2nd July, 1961

'The two sources of Life in Eternity, Hunting and War . . .'
Blake, *Jerusalem.*

And life was good enough, though early, from
eye-corners death's image
seemed to stalk us: a supercilious
discourtesy. This
rankled. Were we not
free, then, being so alive and swift? Where
was deception?
                    In Illinois, surely the gold net
of the morning was spread
only to lighten a boy's heart? In the lightless blue
days in Canada, the unguarded moment like a window
would let in eternity. In Paris, it
seemed possible to make terms
with the terror at the heart of the world.   75

But art
was not enough. There were uneasy
corners of a man's desire, not to be choked
with words: bemused moments
at the edge of evening when the tiger conscience
tensed to flatten the imposing quidnunc
of towns and cultures.
Ha! then, to
turn and face it was work
for a man or hero. Words, after all, were a way
of living: a style of dying (ha, to rescue death
from squalor!) was the improbable
prize.

Turn from the glass; the beautiful man, the
greek paradigm, oh, he grows old. He
sprouts legendary sores not wings, crumbles, dead
duck, athwart his own shadow, or is lost
at sea, spreadeagled on hapless tides. To praise him
is no longer seemly. Turn
from the glass.

Mervyn Morris

The Early Rebels

Time and the changing passions played them tricks,
Killing the shop-soiled resolutions dead.
Gone are the early angry promises
Of rich men squeezed, of capitalists bled.
More adult honesties have straightened ties
And brushed the dinner-jackets clean,
Maturer minds have smelt out fallacies
And redefined what thinkers mean.

Hope drives a chromium symbol now
And smiles a toothpaste passion to the poor,
With colder eloquence explaining how
The young were foolish when they swore
That all those dunghills dank and dreary
Would be replaced by bright new flats:
Good sense was never youthful fury
And rash young promises by brats . . .

'Let's drink a loyal toast to dedication:
We mean the same but youth is past;
We are the fathers of our nation,
The thinking leaders come at last.
Cheers for the faith of simple minds,
Cheers for the love of humble friends;
Love does not alter when it finds
That we have redefined its ends.'

Mervyn Morris

Jukebox

The squeamish, folding their cultured serviettes,
Condemn you, but they do not know
The life that pulses from you, thumping strong
With passion, crude and fake maybe
But speaking plain to many living heartbeats.

What right have these dogmatics earned
To claim the jukebox-lovers do not face
The deeper facts of living?
What Bach may do for them, or Proust,
You do for others who are quite as true;
Imposing your own order, paying on demand,
You make distinctions few dons understand.

Louis Simpson

American Dreams

In dreams my life came toward me,
My loves that were slender as gazelles.
But America also dreams.
Dream, you are flying over Russia.
Dream, you are falling in Asia.

As I look down the street
On a typical sunny day in California
It is my house that is burning
And my dear ones that lie in the gutter
As the American army enters.

Every day I wake far away
From my life, in a foreign country.
These people are speaking a strange language.
It is strange to me,
And strange, I think, even to themselves.

Louis Simpson

New Masters

You were dreaming of the past
And your victory over the German.
But evil comes from within,
And the face of evil varies.
It is not the same as it was last time.

Last time was the tyrant insane?
This time he swears like a cattleman.
He lives by the give and take
Of eyes, hands, cash, the bargain
Struck for a practical life.

Why are you astonished
That men who think only of money
Control you? You were sleeping,
And so it is, you are commanded
By the masters of sensual life.

Vivian Virtue

Columbus

(At his disputed tomb in the Basilica of Santo Domingo)

Where rests the scanty dust we still may doubt,
Whether beneath this, or Havana's dome;
But none can doubt the true unresting home
Of your adventurous spirit. Faring out
With all the voyaging stars and winds in rout,
Beyond horizons of our faith you roam,
Your monument the marmoreal foam,
Your questing spirit an eternal scout.

Those caravels by gnashing waves and rocks
Set on, beat back disaster; savaged oar and mast
From one wild onset to another hurled,
Held on intrepid, weathering the shocks,—
Until their hounded weary keels at last
Won you San Salvador's incredible world.

Derek Walcott

The Glory Trumpeter

Old Eddie's face, wrinkled with river lights
Looked like a Mississippi man's. The eyes,
Derisive and avuncular at once,
Swivelling, fixed me. They'd seen
Too many wakes, too many cathouse nights.
The bony, idle fingers on the valves
Of his knee-cradled horn could tear
Through 'Georgia on my Mind' or 'Jesus Saves'
With the same fury of indifference,
If what propelled such frenzy was despair.

Now, as the eyes sealed in the ashen flesh,
And Eddie, like a deacon at his prayer,
Rose, tilting the bright horn, I saw a flash
Of gulls and pigeons from the dunes of coal
Near my grandmother's barracks on the wharves,
I saw the sallow faces of those men
Who sighed as if they spoke into their graves
About the negro in America. That was when
The Sunday comics, sprawled out on her floor,
Sent from the States, had a particular odour:
The smell of money mingled with man's sweat.

And yet, if Eddie's features held our fate,
Secure in childhood I did not know then
A jesus-ragtime or gut-bucket blues
To the bowed heads of limp, compliant men
Back from the States in their funereal serge,
Black, rusty Homburgs and limp waiters' ties
Molasses accents and lard-coloured eyes
Was Joshua's ram's horn wailing for the Jews
Of patient bitterness and bitter siege.

Now it was that as Eddie turned his back
On our young crowd out feteing, swilling liquor,
And blew, eyes closed, one foot up, out to sea,
His horn aimed at those cities of the Gulf,
Mobile and Galveston and sweetly meted
The horn of plenty through a bitter cup,
In lonely exaltation blaming me
For all whom race and exile have defeated,
For my own uncle in America,
That living there I never could look up.

Ian McDonald

Son Asleep, Aged Six Months

Before our own sleep of passion, dreams, and clocks,
Warm wife and my proud self watch by his sovereign bed.
Over the child our smiling eyes like emperor's shine;
In his warm life our hopes spring tall as spears.
Pray God he finds a destiny well-designed.

Against the terrific future how can he sleep so soft?
He is not golden-armed, he is not tall or strong.
So gently born, so sweetly grown, so calm,
He rests soft beyond birth only half a year
Deathless he must be, no pains will visit him;
He breathes quiet as white leaves of moonlight,
His fist clenches like a young rose in his sleep.
My son's face is serious for peace and good intent,
His small heart is burning like a star.

This is not so, he is not safe forever:
Death rages in man's bones all the days he lives.
My son's not singular, death rages in him too;
Long time to come, long years past this proud present watching
He will find agonies enough, he will be hurt.
The flesh is kingly, but kings' dethronement comes.

Yet let him sleep so soft as this,
Give him some sweet preliminary of life;
Do not warn him too soon of cruelties and sleepless lusts,
The bribery of habits, red wounds, the iron nations' wars
In this raw age of jealous total moods
Which men soon march to order behind dogmatic whims.
We watch and deeply love and we determine this:
Take childhood's time and make a dream of it.

E. M. Roach

The Picture

I would I were Rembrandt, had all that light,
My art his art, my paper for his canvas,
And see her so, to hold her so,
A moment laughing in the running moment.

The wind turns gently through her rust-brown hair
And channels in her hollow cheek; her eyes
Alive with pleasure that her red mouth laughs;
A gesture like a phrase, a chord, a curve.

I would take care to show her in her world
That scorns and envies and outlaws her worth,
The freedom she must live, the gaiety she is,
The whole earth's love and pity she possesses.

I should take care to name the picture 'Harlot'.
Lest those who come, not knowing, but enraptured
By the wild beauty and the goddess gesture
Should say she was the duchess of my heart.

It would not be the first time nor the last
The truth were wronged nor the lie hidden in
The line or colour; the man must love the model,
Or the work comes stillborn from the soul.

Light rises in the mind: it filled Rembrandt's
And warmed him till he died. All that he looked at
Lives; all that he made burns like the sun:
Time cannot blind the vision of his spirit.

Time cannot burn the lovely legends down;
Their golden flame warms history's sodden heart.
Why, all that love and pity had Isolde,
And such a beauty had the Magdalen.

E. M. Roach

The World of Islands

Watch from a journey close to cloud
A shoal of sea-beleagured lands,
Siblings of the glaring sun
Grin their dolphin teeth at heaven.

A difficult country to inherit:
Guilt is humid in the glittering air;
Grafted at every branch the human wood
Blooms a bewildering scent, fruits bitter-sweet;

Indigenous blood still stains the grass;
Dragon's teeth still rattle under root,
And under stone the cold snake's coiled asleep,
Rapt in its murderous dream.

Those whom bondage bit to bone,
Who early learnt to sieve black grief
Through hardihood and song and prayer,
Repaint the tragic mask.
The shattered man sewn in the rock
Arises smiling like the surf,
Reaching to kiss each wind,
Groping to clouds for love.

The drummer with his father's knuckles
Knocks the torrid drum of the sun;
The dancer shakes her castanet the moon
To the loud rhyme of love, calling:
Come, come I am the phoenix Eve,
The mingled wine of the world's grapes;
I am the supple rhythm of the seas;
I recreate the world on islands.

E. M. Roach

I Am The Archipelago

I am the archipelago hope
Would mould into dominion; each hot green island
Buffeted, broken by the press of tides
And all the tales come mocking me
Out of the slave plantations where I grubbed
Yam and cane—where heat and hate sprawled down
Among the cane—my sister sired without
Love or law. In that gross bed was bred
The third estate of colour. And now
My language, history and my names are dead
And buried with my tribal soul. And now
I drown in the groundswell of poverty
No love will quell. I am the shanty town,
Banana, sugar cane and cotton man;
Economies are soldered with my sweat
Here, everywhere; in hate's dominion;
In Congo, Kenya, in free, unfree America.

83

I herd in my divided skin
Under a monomaniac sullen sun
Disnomia deep in artery and marrow.
I burn the tropic texture from my hair;
Marry the mongrel woman or the white;
Let my black spinster sisters tend the church,
Earn meagre wages, mate illegally
Breed secret bastards, murder them in womb,
Their fate is written in unwritten law,
The vogure of colour hardened into custom
In the tradition of the slave plantation.

Patrick Fernando

Andromache

Let a hundred Hectors meet the worst of fates and die,
And let the Trojan plains brim with blood and make
Wine-dark flood for another Grecian fleet.
Let household gods, charred and nude, awake
And work revenge, while kindred skulls crackle and burst;
Let another greater Ilium rise out of the dust
And fall.
I shall not cry, nor fear, nor hate,
For feelings drawn too tight have snapped, and crushed
The rich concord of joy and pain and bred a heartless woman
Born on the hot, black bed of war.
Here come the Greeks romping merrily
On the huge reaped heap of gold Troy;
Their toy horse stands and stares, the belly door still open,
The womb just delivered of future history.
Hearts that bore ten years the sound of blood and bodies broken,
Melted at a child's trick—a little joke.
And a city wept and shrank and ended up in smoke.

Play, tin soldiers, play; play while the sun is high.
Pause not to pity me, for why
Should children at their summer play
Regard a lone ridiculous leaf
Hanging limp and forgotten
In a winter wood?

David Jonklaas

Matador to his Love—Death

I am always ready for you,
Carefully waiting,
My ravenhaired lover.
I have never been afraid of you,
I studiously waited
For you, my eager one.

85

In the silence before the corrida
It is to you I pray,
My palecheeked mistress.
In the rumble of the arena
It is your lips I watch,
You coquette, smiling.

In the hush of caught breath
It is your feet I mark
Fearfully pattering.
Through the dust that smarts senses
It is your shoulders that weave
And always beckon.

With the rising blood of the song!
Oh, do not drop your fan!
Whirl that mantilla!
At the crescendo, so long,
Hold me not to your eye,
Faithful one.

Then, at the flash! we kiss,
I take your sword,
Searing lover,
Then I sigh myself to your feet,
I clasp your body,
Rolling over.

Michael Ondaatje

Description is a Bird

In the afternoon
while the sun twists down
they come piggle piggle piggle
all around the air.
Under clouds of horses turning black
looking on earth
the sand swallows turn
quick and gentle as wind.
All virtuoso performances
that presume a magnificent audience.

Skating on wings
their tails sensitive rudders
the leader will fling his neck back
and like a bad hound
turn thinner than whims.
Like God the other follows
anticipating every twist
—the betrayals of a feather.

For them no thumping wing beat of a crow
they bounce on a breath like stones on water
and scatter with the discipline of a watch.

Michael Ondaatje

Over the Garden Wall

'We've been watching you over the garden wall
    for hours,
The sky is darkening like a stain,
Something is going to fall like rain
    and it won't be flowers.'

My mother, while caressing camels,
had her left breast bitten off.
So I was weaned on half a body.

In spite of this I've no objections
to camels, one hump or two,
and I like their quivering jaws
that crunch bones
and stones with equal ease,

while the Canadian wolf,
with his flailing
double-jointed legs,
is to my mind
the most awesome beast on this continent.

My appreciation includes several breeds:
hornery skinned buffaloes,
oozing leopards,
scattered crows,
black-magic spiders,
and Dodo birds.

87

When taking in a zoo therefore
it seems absurd that these beasts
who look intelligent enough for civil life
are made hostages in our society.

I mean
the infamous camel
would not look ridiculous in a felt hat,
pigs could trot like angels down a high street,
a leopard in a two-seater
would look just as refined as Hugh Hefner,
and their gaudy, glorious, Elizabethan-like dress
would certainly liven up our major cities
and impress visiting communists no end.

But instead, in this day and age,
in spite of warnings by Daphne du Maurier,
we find the 'potamus barred from public swimming-pools,
and a vulture calmly resting on a traffic light
would undoubtedly be shot, very messily,
by the first policeman who spotted him.

Gaminin Seneviratne

An Encounter

Everyone is not young as Yevtushenko
says he is. . . .

It is easy to be young
in a nation which is getting butter for a change
and open-necked shirts and pullovers
made (as they're designed to be)
a size too large;

when even the heavy machinery's begun
sprouting lilies in the sky.

Sometimes
you too seem young, meaning
that I become aware
of a confrontation. And again I do not know
whether to be young is here
the same thing as the young
in raw Russia
applauding Yevtushenko, understand,
where to be an artist of good family
only to Kruschev, and such,
seems significant,

or in London where
labour is so respectable.

It is easy to be young
in a nation which is said to be only
forty-seven years old
when one is not yet forty and does not quite remember
the birthpangs, and the virtues
of one generation only need
to be lived down.

Taner Baybars

Constancy

There's something that we should be thankful for,
praise the smoothness of our skins,
the versatility of Earth's hide,
and creatures that come therefrom,
the plants that grow from within,
the different seasons,
yes, praise the different seasons
and be thankful. Because the Sun is small.

And a small star radiates at a constant rate,
cannot burn or freeze,
thank god, thank
the small Star, our Sun,
the giver of all healthy seasons.

A bigger star would have been your end
supposing we had a beginning, you and I.
Can you imagine: the seed would freeze
in the soil at night, and during the day
you would have to climb on a geranium
to touch its red petals.
Not to speak of the rest.

Yes, it's marvellous to have a constant sun.
If you don't try to emulate your predecessor
this one will be more than enough for you.

Taner Baybars

Do the Dying Cry?

The balcony shakes, the wrought-iron bars
melt as she cries, holding them,
I holding my father's hand
down in the street, looking up, seeing her
mouth swallow her face, and behind her
a silent room. Behind the balcony
with wrought-iron bars.

She's dying. Probably she's dead, my father
says, tries to walk away. I cannot ask
who is dying, who is probably dead.

The carob tree begins to move where the leaves
are freest. One leaf touches the balcony;
and from the hill a dog's barking
imitates her dying-cry—the wind carries
both to the sea, drops them there,
returns to the balcony, to me under it,
holding my father's hand with a question:

Do the dying cry on balconies, do they resent
this sudden misplacement?—Come, now,
you are old enough to know: her *mother* must be
dead, behind that balcony, in that silent room.

Lenrie Peters
Consider a Snail

Consider a snail.
You would have
thought its movements
slimy. No, circumspect.
Its towering oblivion
grounded in humility
irritates the idea
of energy. Ten years
to reach some green
morsel on Mars
is nothing to a snail; morally.
Morsel and chlorophyll
will wait embittered
a generation or two
till some waif snail
snaps it up with
less guts; more luck.

Snails fear rapaciousness
prefix for madness,
like lightning ambling
through the sky. Where
will it strike or die?
Snails are unerringly
sane and dry.

Let rough winds
carry phantoms into tomorrow.
Winds to hang on
naked deserted trees; dateless.
Snails linger obscurely
in the sand, hedges, half shadows
essentially fresh, essentially alive.
Eternally striving, that's all!

Lenrie Peters

Wings My Ancestors Used

Wings my ancestors used
to fly from oppression, slavery,
tincture of skin, arid birth and death,
hang limp on my shoulders
with guilt of the oppressor.
I am a tamed eagle,
no serpent in my claws.
They saw the world inviolate
created in seven days.
Amazedly I have inherited
the will to oppression,
the love of it, the anger
staring out of darkness.

Today I give my blood for venison victory,
tomorrow another's will wet the earth,
libation to saints and freedom.
History cordially accepts it
as if ordained, but history is not inevitable.
Breezes from the past feather my curls,
ancient animosities gnawing like giant bulldozers
compress my passages into a phallic stem,
cycle of stagnation beginning at the end;
like science, exploding benefits
in a million worlds of chaos; computing eternity of chaos.

I would believe though I don't quite know what.
It would be easy to believe in something,
quench the thirst, make it up with nature,
Chardin; like cosmic diplomats
comprising the cold war of the soul. I would believe.
I see the stars adorned,
immensity of chaos in space,
revolutions of desire and object faced together.

I would say: the end of all things is eternal
and life makes living true.
Guilt-edged present invests the future,
rain and plant-growth intermingled
diadem of knowledge, profusion of time possibilities
shield my aching eyes from the sun
rub my sore gums with crystal salt.

I will go alone darkly till I have done.
Ignorant laughter, revenge
pass through me like memory,
nibble my breath in gasps
then fall away like an outsize pair of pants.
Naked my conviction of doubt,
primitive with Socrates and others
wandering bitterly alone, dying
wandering eternally in doubt.

There may be purer worlds to come,
days crisp with settling snow and mushroom clouds
mating in the park leaves postured in protest
world without conscience expiating guilt,
protons whirling in energy
as befits a chain reaction.
That is the substance of things,
the guidance is in me; in me.

But my blood is saturate with opium
smoking wastefully away
like the passion of summer days.
Sausage knees crawl in Alabama,
Vietnam, Berlin; at the colour of my skin
religion, at the sound of contest,
while voices rage with destruction:
I am a trustee for the future
before I have lived out today.
That is the substance of things,
the guidance is in me.

Jawa Apronti

Entirely Uprooted?

It's said that all Ghanaians have a village
But I'll soon have none—
And yet it doesn't move me.

I went down there the other day to see
The Devastation.
Yet it didn't move me.
Not for me the deep romantic attachment
To a sentimental ancestral home.

I first heard of the Devastation three years ago
And my last visit was five years ago—
Yet it didn't move me.
My curiosity, even,
Wasn't stirred enough to send me there.
The floods came again and
Ate the new rims of the village.

I heard of it and said
'If only this will wipe away their wickedness:
The wickedness that has cost us many noble sons.'
When I went, the heart of the village
Still beat—but with a dying cadence,
Faintly, faintly. . . .
And when the whole village
Dives
And the ghosts of my ancestors die,
Will it move me?

I will be curious, of course, to see the new lake.
Yes, curious to see it when I have time.
And concerned
To see if my aunts have moved
Safely to Grandfather's roof seven miles away.
For he left this wicked village
Twenty years ago, after the very first flood
Had eaten up his house and others'.

Ever since then I have considered his new abode
—The single house—
As my 'village', and not
The ancestral one.

95

And so the saying will stand
That all Ghanaians have a village.
I will have none
And yet I'll be
A Ghanaian.

Kwesi Brew

Ancestral Faces

They sneaked into the limbo of time.
But could not muffle the gay jingling
Bells on the frothy necks
Of the sacrificial sheep that limped and nodded after them.
They could not hide the moss on the bald pates
Of their reverent heads,
And the gnarled barks of the *wawa* trees;
Nor the rust on the ancient state-swords;
Nor the skulls studded with grinning cowries.
They could not silence the drums,
The fibre of their souls and ours—
The drums that whisper to us behind black sinewy hands.
They gazed,
And sweeping like white locusts through the forests
Saw the same men, slightly wizened,
Shuffle their sandalled feet to the same rhythms.
They heard the same words of wisdom uttered
Between puffs of pale blue smoke.
They saw us,
And said: They have not changed!

Kwesi Brew

Our Palm Tree Strength

The short days, breathing
In sharp painful spurts,
Die on the wings of the silk-cotton
Clouds homing past
The unthatched roof of humanity.

The sleep-roaring dove
Shuts its golden eyelids
Against the darkness of the night.

And still I sit here in the dust
Struggling to understand
The world and its words.
And so I have sometimes cast
A hopeful glance over the shoulders of those
Whose hoes have helped
A friend to till a thorny ground
And wondered whether to look
In fear upon the past or to rejoice;
To rejoice that we have achieved so much,
That so much has escaped
The eyes of the gods who hold
The rod of punishment;
That the red-clay kitchens
Of our ancestral homes still
Teem with the feasts of the year.

The song we sing shall be
Of our faith in humanity
And the upward surge of our hopes.
Like the waves we shall surge forward
And spray the tired faces of the gods
With the cool refreshing breakers of our spirits.

Kwesi Brew

The Dry Season

The year is withering; the wind
Blows down the leaves;
Men stand under eaves
And overhear the secrets
Of the cold dry wind,
Of the half-bare trees.

The grasses are tall and tinted,
Straw-gold hues of dryness,
And the contradicting awryness
Of the dusty roads a-scatter
With pools of colourful leaves,
With ghosts of the dreaming year.

And soon, soon the fires,
The fires will begin to burn,

The hawk will flutter and turn
On its wings and swoop for the mouse,
The dogs will run for the hare,
The hare for its little life.

Kofi Dei-Anang

By Air to Germany

Up here speed became insensible. Only
The brisk knowledge of a thousand miles
Traversed in two extended hours.
The mathematics of speed slows down
Hearts leaping to the zest of distance covered.

Up here, eyes, too, were deceptive
Watching the landscape snail;
And ears, unpricking, sleepy to the hum
Daisy-chained one minute to another
On strings of idle words.

It took, of course, much longer
Twenty years ago when our elders
Crouched in draughts, and darkness
Trailed their aeroplanes through the vault of heaven;

Refining for our time a time-defying ritual
Caked-black in the blood of years:
When life was bought with near-total death;
When infinite extension of patience gave birth
To disciplined intension of communal hate.

Kofi Dei-Anang

I Saw No Marble Columns Here

I saw no marble columns here;
Pentelic stone remains unheard-of;
Olive groves are not to be seen here
	Spreading a sun-etched net
	Across the turquoise sky.

There are no winters, springs and autumns;
Only absence of rain and absence of sun
And the star-spattered velvet night sky.

I saw no tourist-layered beaches—
Holiday towns remain unthought-of;
Music halls are yet to be built here
    Echoing gossamer strains
    Of night-mist-combing song.

There are no concerts and drama festivals,
Only the impromptu throb of drums, and song
In sweat-drenched unison under burning skies.

This is my home;
Where columns are tree-trunks
Swaying leafy capitals in the afternoon haze;
More stately than Doric columns, but
Obeying only nature's geometry.

In the market places
Black babies at their mothers' breasts,
And children round the fufu bowls
Huddled like suckling puppies.

And everyone I met
Asked why I failed to greet him;
And everyone I knew
Came at inconvenient hours
To welcome me from exile;
Uncles, aunts, and cousins thrice-removed
Sat round and heard my travel tales.
And I was glad.

John Okai

The Pioneer

I
Expect me . . . my dear mother—
Expect me . . . but only
When you shall see me
Coming;

I am still in the wilderness
Alone,
But do not worry because
Of me.
The fruits of the tall trees,
The waters
Of the silent springs and streams
Feed me.
From the moon and sun I have
My light,
For my bed and pillow I approach
The leaves,
The animals clothe me with
Their skins,
The birds sing for me—this is all
I need . . .
And our native forests are rich
In these,
And in forests, our native land
Is rich.
I would have told you this:
'Your memory
Has made me endure the sunrays'
Bullying,
The biting of the ants and the
Cold night'.
This is not so—the elephant's skin
Is mine,
The hare has lent me her feet,
The nose
Of the bat is mine; mine is the
Lion's heart.
To me has been lent the neck of
The giraffe,
The stomach of the camel and the
Zebra's hair.
I speak the language of the antelope
And leopard.
Yet expect me . . . my dear mother
Expect me . . . but only
When you shall see me
Coming.

II
Expect me . . . my dear mother
Expect me . . . but only
When you shall see me

Coming;

Do not allow my sisters to sit
By the roadside
Expecting me; don't allow them into
Any bush
Looking out for me . . . don't allow them
To hide
In any corner thinking and sorrowing
Over my absence;
Don't let my sisters have a cause
To weep
Otherwise they shall cry the more,
Thinking
Of how I would have consoled them
In my arms
Had I been there with them at home;
Do not
Put any food or fruit aside
For me;
Give to my sisters and brothers gifts
Meant for me.
But during libation you could call
My name,
And when answering questions on
Our family.
Expect me . . . my dear mother
Expect me . . . but only
When you shall see me coming.

III
Expect me . . . my mother
Expect me . . . but only
When you shall see me
Coming;
Tell my sisters to build
The hearth—
I shall soon carry home
The firewood.
Tell them to reconstruct it
A thousand times,
Not minding the destructive
Erosive rains;
Our father has built for us
A house,
And I must furnish it into
A home;
To the pot I must return home
With water,
For the hoestick I must mould
A blade,

101

For the floors I must collect
A broom,
For the courtyard I must carve
Out some stools,
For the mortar I must find
A head,
For the rooms I must weave
Some mats,
For the spears I must melt some
Spearheads,
And teach my sisters how
To man them.
I am the male among you;
I am our father's first son.
Expect me . . . my dear mother
Expect me . . . but only
When you shall see me coming.

Frank Kobina Parkes

After the Holocaust

Let us build new homesteads
New dreams to decorate these ruins
Let us weave fresh rafters from rescued stalks
Let us start all over again

The past is a pitiless dream
A dread nightmare, you may remember, which stared
Deep into our fearless eyes
We gave it glance for glance
Frown for frown
Fouler word for filthy word
And when it kept on staring
Like a senseless imbecile
We lost our minds completely
We braced ourselves to self-assertion
To knock this beast over
And so redeem our peace.

And that, you may remember,
Was the storm clouds breaking over us
And death marching in
And flowering fields laid low
102   And children in the womb with them

Now we look back to the pity of the nightmare
Not being anywhere near at all
And to sad awakening that our stare
Had been nowhere but into blank brotherly eyes
Seized by delirium like ourselves
And that, had the black storm only given us
A moment's chance,
And not struck just then . . .

But the past is horrific reality.

Frank Kobina Parkes

Apocalypse at Birth

In the last days,
Strange sights shall visit the earth,
Sights that may turn to blood the moon,
This sun to midnight—in the last days.

But now, when swords are not yet ploughshares,
And spears still spears
Hearken you, my little ones.

If walking, shaded by the mango tree,
Or running naked, scorched by the blazing sun,
You aught perceive
Now, while the arrow remains arrow,
And the miracle of spears and pruning hooks
Still remains an unseen miracle
Remember, my little ones,
If perchance your infant feet do slide,
And you find yourselves in some mysterious dungeon
Of black vengeful Sasabonsam
In realms where dogs make speech,
And horns adorn the human front;
Where mermaids in their skirts of silvery scales
And chattering seabeasts flout mankind—
If in this strange sub-human realm
Your eyes fall on a stone, a hard black stone,
Lifeless and muddy, that has grown a beard,
Pray children, pass silently by.
Ask no questions.
For you are face to face with the first days
And the beginning and the end are one.

And in the end shall strange sights visit earth,
Stones shall be turned to men
And men to stones.
Sparrows beget eagles
And sand become good grain.

So children,
If perchance you see a hare that roars
Or an ape perched in a palanquin,
Look on in silence. Quickly pass it by.
Quickly.

E. Archie Winful

Waste

I am the cathedral that Jack never built;
I am the river-bed choked with silt;
I am the unscored symphony, the unchoired hymn;
I am the tragedy with no hero's part, the dim
Oxygen-starved spark that never burst into flame;
The cell that failed to multiply into a name;
I am the soldier with no foe to hate,
No native land, no insulated state;
I am the pyramid with no catacomb
Of mummied Pharoahs whom no dreams of doom
Disturb, assured of physical survival!
I am She that missed the bridegroom's arrival—
Thought too late of the oil that burns in the lamp;
I am the misdealt letter with no stamp,
Whose intention and value are suspect;
I am the Christ's and Buddha's elect
Who treats with Pharisees and editors
For that which boils the pot but burns the potter's
Fingers; I am the unsolved riddle of the Sphinx
That gives no headache to the great; some links
Perhaps there are in me with this ethos,
To which my dissolution would be no loss!

Deb Kumar Das

The Space-man's Travel

The ocean's edge is end to all except
Wind, lemming, or orbiting spaceman.

Only wind or lemming can attempt
The void beyond horizon's darkest line:

Only spaceman wilfully define
His act of travel in that deeper void.

Spaceman's truth is what wind tells the lemming.
In void where travel becomes identity
No piece of world is trapped in blueblind sky:

All oceans pass endlessly in step
Spaced only by the winking of the sun
That marks the edge of day from shadow night.

No spaceman's instrument speaks journey's end
Of beginning, in the goldfish bowl
Silence in which stars and oceans float.

What spaceman sees beyond the ocean's edge,
What only wind can whisper to dead lemming,
That starquiet passing above a sky's blue roof
That makes a mirage of the world's endings.

Nissim Ezekiel

Poet, Lover, Birdwatcher

To force the pace and never to be still
Is not the way of those who study birds
Or women. The best poets wait for words.
The hunt is not an exercise of will
But patient love relaxing on a hill
To note the movement of a timid wing;
Until the one who knows that she is loved
No longer waits but risks surrendering—
In this the poet finds his moral proved,
Who never spoke before his spirit moved.

The slow movement seems, somehow, to say much more.

To watch the rarer birds, you have to go
Along deserted lanes and where the rivers flow
In silence near the source, or by a shore
Remote and thorny like the heart's dark floor.
And there the women slowly turn around,
Not only flesh and bone but myths of light
With darkness at the core, and sense is found
By poets lost in crooked, restless flight,
The deaf can hear, the blind recover sight.

Nissim Ezekiel

Night of the Scorpion

I remember the night my mother
was stung by a scorpion. Ten hours
of steady rain had driven him
to crawl beneath a sack of rice.
Parting with his poison—flash
of diabolic tail in the dark room—
he risked the rain again.
The peasants came like swarms of flies
and buzzed the Name of God a hundred times
to paralyse the Evil One.
With candles and with lanterns
throwing giant scorpion shadows
on the mud-baked walls
they searched for him: he was not found.
They clicked their tongues.
With every moment that the scorpion made
his poison moved in Mother's blood, they said.
May he sit still, they said.
May the sins of your previous birth
be burned away tonight, they said.
May your suffering decrease
the misfortunes of your next birth, they said.
May the sum of evil
balanced in this unreal world
against the sum of good
become diminished by your pain.
May the poison purify your flesh
of desire, and your spirit of ambition,
they said, and they sat around
on the floor with my mother in the centre,
the peace of understanding on each face.

More candles, more lanterns, more neighbours
more insects, and the endless rain.

My mother twisted through and through
groaning on a mat.
My father, sceptic, rationalist,
trying every curse and blessing,
powder, mixture, herb and hybrid.
He even poured a little paraffin
upon the bitten toe and put a match to it.
I watched the flame feeding on my mother.
I watched the holy man perform his rites
to tame the poison with an incantation.
After twenty hours
it lost its sting.

My Mother only said
Thank God the scorpion picked on me
and spared my children.

P. Lal

In Memoriam: Jawaharlal Nehru

What hurts is not the passing in the night.
Rooted trees dig deeper as they grow.
Neither the fading of what was once bright.
Embers glow brighter in minds that know.
Not the bowing of a proud head.
Such sadness is every day's delight.
Neither the memory of noble words uttered
In the course of a lifetime's noble fight.

Only a fine disappearance,
Fine feeling in an age of doubt,
A sculptured face, eyes in gentle trance,
Voice that breathed nobility about.
Only the dying of a nuance,
Refined passion forever snuffed out.

R. Parthasarathy

The Leader

The streets overflowed: the traffic
came to a halt minutes before
the limousine came into view.

107

The town held its breath: children
whispered. A policeman dropped
his baton. A crowd strained at the leash.

Above, a crow flew in absolute
freedom. From the airport
to the city a people waited.
Paper flags were waved, slogans
chanted. He had changed the face
of the country (you laugh), yes,
with speeches and brave promises
and eternal vigilance and all that.
When he appeared waving
a hand he seemed tired and yawned.

Gieve Patel

On Killing a Tree

It takes much time to kill a tree,
Not a simple jab of the knife
Will do it. It has grown
Slowly consuming the earth,
Rising out of it, feeding
Upon its crust, absorbing
Years of sunlight, air, water,
And out of its leprous hide
Sprouting leaves.

So hack and chop
But this alone won't do it.
Not so much pain will do it.
The bleeding bark will heal
And from close to the ground
Will rise curled green twigs,
Miniature boughs
Which if unchecked will expand again
To former size.

No,
The root has to be pulled out—
Out of the anchoring earth;
It has to be roped, tied,
And pulled out—snapped out
Or pulled out entirely,
Out from the earth-cave,

And the strength of the tree exposed,
The source, white and wet,
The most sensitive, hidden
For years inside the earth.
Then the matter
Of scorching and choking
In sun and air,
Browning, hardening,
Twisting, withering,
And then it is done.

Tilottama Rajan

A Painter

Your fact became their fiction.

Winter set in thick paint
cleaving to canvas
black gnarled branches
scarring the sky
in calculating texture that defined your life.

The tangled roots heaved themselves
out of the ground
loosing a stooping figure in their clutch,
a figure bound unwillingly
by roots his eyes denied,
translating them into an eyeless labyrinth.

Your tree loomed in the present of your canvas
against a background of dull Hiroshima,
history grappling with geography,
history grappling with science:
man who wrought creation
bore destruction, now
stoops over his footprints, face averted
from the heavy roots that bind.

That was your greatness: that you showed
man's weakness. That you showed man.

A. K. Ramanujan

Happiness: After Some Anthropology

I'm happy, sir,

      that shields of painted cane, the
        sociology
      of Anglo-Indian rum,
      wooden drum,

      carved human head
      and the xylophone or
      the charisma of brahmins

      and the ritual use
      of bark-cloth and silver
      and the two figurines

      of the Shaven Ass
      styles of tattooing
      spiders on the waist

      of the infertile wife
      or animal masks that grin
      in tiger-moth colours

      with white and yellow lines
      round a hole for a mouth
      or masks that simply grin

      in olive-green
      among red circles
      for eyes, do not yet

exclude
a look

at the face
of the happy widow

of our varicose
cook, nor another look

at mushrooms, those
parasol mobs

in the reeking crotch
of rotting timber

bought for my uncle's
very carefully

imagined
houses.

A. K. Ramanujan

The Fall

Falling,
I think of a man falling,
a plummet in a parachute
that will take half his life to sprout and take root,
while he, a mere body, a surrender,
a will-less plunge into the downward
below his blindness, cannot find a word
for a curse, nor an eye for a hook.
Then
the sudden catch
of grace,
of finding that even face-
less men have fingers in a row;
and the slow, all-too-slow
unfurling
of help behind his back,
segment by segment, of a silk bowl
held upside down to hold the pouring howl
of a pack of winds,
a grip on the crotch
of his braces, a mothercat's teeth
on the scruff of her kitten,
the very air a sheath
of safety
for the floating, the amniotic floating without hands
into an exhilaration
of larks, a man
amassed for all the darks
now a-dangle
at the raying threads and spangles
of ecstasy.

> The careful calculus
> of the retarded fall draws
> the earth-map under the lenses,

111

projects the trees, blanches
to a blur the contour lines
isolating the needle-pines
till he almost begins
to count
till he reaches
his end, the Ground,
all his limbs but scratches
on the rubble,
misses by the mere limp of a foot
the flower behind the ear
of a prickly pear
in the violence of the dragging wind,
a fallen rider held by his reins
to a flight of horses.

He finds his feet.
Sparse, alien houses
watch.
Some windows
slam on a flash: fieldglasses
on a hill
without the tallness of a tree or the wideness
of a street.

Pradip Sen

The Man on My Back

The man on my back
Hates my guts,
Gives me no rest
And spurns all I love best.

The man on my back
Tears my dreams apart
And ravages my heart;
Give him enough rope
He'll strangle every hope.

The man on my back,
He's a killer—
Kills the boy in me,
And the man that would be;
The man on my back,
My replica.

Khadambi Asalache

High Mountain

You stand like a sculptured idol,
Your face untaken by surrounding passions.
You watch with unconcerned indifference
These storms assembling in conference.
You show a blue front, blind
To the sky's changing moods,
To swaying nature's armies,
Drifts of rivers, noises from skies
Flooding and shaking their way.
You stand high, modest
A dreamer, an unannounced king
Poising your unprotected cheeks
Against this kingdom of streams, winds
Weaving bent stories in their wings.
You wait, patient, silent
In midnight hours; your crown head gleams
Bright to moonbeam-waken owls
To reveal their hidden speed,
From storm-laden clouds
Shaking treetops from a pretentious smile
To soak their leaves into submission.
Your silence is like a shadow
Moving to touch the dead and the unborn,
Showing an image, an immortal sight.
You, high mountain, fluent with changing times,
Briefed in the spiral ways of the world,
Noising their presence in a passing sport;
Make me faithful unto your lone visions
To stand high above these gathering storms.

Khadambi Asalache

Fencesitters

They come on the screen of one's mind
Inverted, letters coming in succession; titles
Cancelled yet illuminated. Their words glide
On transparent wings. They are angels of flattery
Who rise and fall with the speed of mercury
And return into the bulb when the weather is cold.

113

They walk on pads in a dry season;
They colour and discolour themselves when a storm
Uproots tottering totems of heroes
Thrown into darkness. Later you find them in form
Climbing up hills, proclaiming aloud
'We've done it again, stopped the terrible catastrophe.'

Fencesitters are fish on a wrack of sand;
Chameleons wearing weatherproof suits, made to measure;
A false alarm permanently on guard
Unaware of a hidden monster, a caterpillar
Camouflaged in a shell, growing slowly
As it eats the roots of the shaky fence.

Bevinda Noronha

The Tide

Like a piece of driftwood on the shore,
I wait;
Like a seashell cupping unshed tears,
I wait—
Till the fisherman counts his catch,
Till the light merges into darkness,
Till the birds are seen no more
And the sea murmurs, now softly,
Now harshly, now softly;

And I wait,
With my hands clasped around my knees,
My toes buried in the sand,
My hair blowing in the wind,
My face wet;
And I wait,
Asking, *Why, why should this be?*

But the sea overwhelms me,
Sweeping away all doubts, all fears,
Making all shrink in humility
Before this overpowering immensity;
And I am dwarfed into insignificance,
Like a grain of sand,

Like a piece of driftwood
Left on this desolate shore
With the ebbing of the tide,
Alone, unrecognisable
In this vast world
Of sky, of sea, of living creatures.

Like a seashell, now empty,
Echoing the murmur of the sea,
Nothing is left now
But a memory,
Nothing is left
But the salt clinging close
To my skin.

David Rubadiri

Ogunoba's Talking Drum

Scratching fussily
Like a chicken looking for seeds
Into the heart of Ibadan
Where Ogunoba lived,
Like traitors
Daggers-drawn
Yet afraid
        (of what?)
We knew not
We were looking for a talking drum.

We sat,
Dutifully broke a kola nut;
Two worlds
East and West—
Both African.

A drum,
We wanted a drum—
Just a drum
Like tourists crying
For a cowrie shell.

Was this a cry,
A longing
Or a conquering wish?
Groping in the dark
Wishing to say
Something
Infinitely impulsive—
Childishly silly?

It came
With a message
That scuffled time beyond time.
There was bargaining,
Mere talk beyond time
A form without meaning,
A bed cover for truth;
Ogunoba broke into tears
Blessing the drum
That would 'fly'
To the East—
A prayer

Spanning ages of definitive African politics.

David Rubadiri

Kampala Beggar

Dark twisted form
Of shreds and cunning
Crawling with an inward twinkle
At the agonies of Africa.

Praying and pricing
Passers by
As in black and white
Jingle pennies past;

A hawk's eye
Penetrates to the core
On a hot afternoon
To pick the victims
That with a mission
Dare not look at
This conflict.

A dollar drops,
An Indian sulk
Passively avoids—
I am stabbed to the core;
Pride rationally injured.

In the orbits of our experience
Our beggarness meets
With the clang of symbols,
Beggarly we understand
As naturally we both know
The Kampala beggar
Is wise—

David Rubadiri

A Negro Labourer in Liverpool

I passed him
Slouching on dark backstreet pavements
Head bowed—

Taut, haggard and worn.
A dark shadow amidst dark shadows.

I stared;
Our eyes met
But on his dark negro face
No sunny smile,
No hope or a longing for a hope promised;
Only the quick cowed dart of eyes
Piercing through impassive crowds
Searching longingly for a face
That might flicker understanding.

This is him—
The negro labourer in Liverpool
That from his motherland
With new hope
Sought for an identity—
Grappled to clutch the fire of manhood
In the land of the free.

Will the sun
That greeted his nativity
Ever shine again?
Not here—
Here his hope is the shovel,
And his fulfilment resignation.

David Rubadiri

An African Thunderstorm

From the west
Clouds come hurrying with the wind
Turning sharply
Here and there
Like a plague of locusts
Whirling,
Tossing up things on its tail
Like a madman chasing nothing.

Pregnant clouds
Ride stately on its back,
Gathering to perch on hills
Like sinister dark wings;
The wind whistles by
And trees bend to let it pass.

In the village
Screams of delighted children
Toss and turn
In the din of the whirling wind,
Women—
Babies clinging on their backs—
Dart about
In and out
Madly;
The wind whistles by
Whilst trees bend to let it pass.

Clothes wave like tattered flags
Flying off
To expose dangling breasts
As jagged blinding flashes
Rumble, tremble, and crack
Amidst the smell of fired smoke
And the pelting march of the storm.

Ee Tiang Hong

The Loan

The terms are more or less fixed,
Payable—you won't feel it—
By instalments,

Say monthly, with effect from
The first moon
Of your beauty.

Therefore you have the choice:
Settle the matter
With grace, or

Publish the transaction,
Expose the catch,
And resign, or,

Finally, though unsound proposition,
And only in the last resort,
Call off the deal,

Coward.

Ee Tiang Hong

On the Death of a Friend in a Distant Country

The morning papers announced his death.
There was nothing more to be said about it;
Only a matter of time and someone's turn
To make the exit.

We felt sorry, of course,
As we would for anything we did not wish
To lose—an old friend,
Dog, cat, house, or the favourite club we cheered.
And for a time we unearthed his living days
Presenting them in a kinder light

(The least we could do
Now he would never come our way again),
Not a soul dissenting, or thinking to deny
Its charity in the sentiments,
It would not be in keeping with the mood
Of the hour now he would never come our way
Again, like a long lost friend,
(Or like a pest, sometimes?).
It would not be in keeping with the mood
Of our anticipating the day we would
Wish the same kindness
And turning aside from the truth.

I would not like to see my friend again
In the flesh bereft of a dignity,
(Death after all is prosaic
Calling for detachment,
The funeral makes the poetry),
I would not like to feel
The faintest trace of a resentment
(What is the point of it all?)
Lingering, like a bad taste in the mouth.

Goh Poh Seng

The History of War

The urge to kill resides in the soul
like barbs that can scratch the sole
of an impalpable sky

The urge to kill can breed wildly,
unleashing violence that was
secretly gestating in sick minds

A start somewhere soon becomes an obsession
inciting a whole populace to destroy, to go
assaulting an already stricken countryside

And even you, a fair and frail child,
with one facile sweep of your hand
maul to its quiet death a tiny fly.

A. Samad Said

Embers

The time will positively come
to the eyes and the heart,
the hope will positively be achieved,
glowing in the heart of the fire.

For this world, this song.

Promises need not be honoured.
The passing wind is not a friend,
the passing wind, the breath of Satan,
promising the climax of destruction.

For this world, this song.

Three wishes, one beloved,
three bones bleached white,*
three hopes, one beautiful,
three revenges, all red.

For this world, this song.

Morning comes to faded eyes.
The only news is of blood.
Who will fly, who will fly to the moon
will not be asked in the blackness of hell.

For this world, this song.

Man will positively fall
on the scorched earth and the burning sea.
Everything will positively writhe,
from the buds to the roots.

For this world, this song.

Tonight there is darkness in my breast.
Everything is afire—everything, yes.

This morning men pray,
the reflection of sin on their brows.

(Translated from the Malayan by
Abdullah Majid and Oliver Rice)

---

* *There is a Malay saying: 'Better white bones than white eyes.'*
It means, approximately, 'Better to die in the attempt than to live
on in unhappiness.'

Mohamad Haji Salleh

Home

Home is the place where the diseased world dies at the door,
where the floor and carpet are worn by familiar feet,
where you can close your eyes and nobody says you are blind.

Home is where you don't have to be polite and sing cane-sweet
song to coat bitterness,
where familiarity accepts you in its security,
where you know that love still breathes somewhere,
where your wife and children keep the other half of you.

When the rain broadcasts the glass face of the fields and moves
the tidemark of the canals,
when you do not know where to go,
home is where they never say 'no'.

The small cottage that sits cosily under the palms,
the atap, brown with time and age hangs to the field,
the complaining hinges and wet stairs,
home is you
and where you hope to die.

M. Shanmughalingam

From a Lighthouse

(For E.T.H.)

I'm a lighthouse
A lighthouse that's
Fused.

I'm a dark house
A was, a has been, an also
Shone.

I'm a heavy house
Broad crow feet roots and thin
Waist.

123

I'm a louse house
A sorry, excuse me, I beg your pardon
Mouse.

I'm a jilt edged security house
An unsociable, stubborn, stay put
House.

I'm a no house
No place in the sea house
Functionless.

Edwin Thumboo

Ahmad

And there is anger
In that bronze patience
Tied to the murmur of his fingers.
Those speaking eyes,
Squatting on me,
Take up my educated helplessness
Against his communal gestures.
An apologetic fidget in the chair
Adjusts his harshness.

He is a son of the soil who roves
The outskirts of our jungle;
He is our brother who moves
With the sun so easily.

Still,
His eyes have strange fires.
Will there be time,
For us, for me,
Groping for a neutral gentleness,
To reach him without burning,
To lift into laughter?

Wong May

Study of a Millionairess: Still Life

Pluck away all its fingers and legs.
We want only the crab's face which is its torso,
unbroken mask,
two lashless eyes
signalling
from the quick.

So the paralysed old woman
with a big yellow cat on her lap
watches her daughters and grandsons
preparing crabs
for the birthday of the Prosperity Goddess,
who is said to be fond of red.

The youngest peeps into the cauldron,
disillusioned because there isn't
any magic like the green-red apples,
while the cat sits washing its face,
patient like any God-child,
moistening its fishy eyes.

So the paralysed old woman
watches her daughters and grandsons
eating crabs (from their nails).
The aged is supposed to be like the Goddess,
to be feasted and fed on the colour of the heart,
while the two lashless eyes,
signalling and signalling,
are red and tired.

Arthur Yap Chior Hiong

A Scroll Painting

The mountains are hazy with timeless passivity,
while clouds diffuse and fill the entire top half
sprawling monotonously in the left-hand corner
before bumping daintily into a bright red parakeet,

perched suicide-like on a beautifully gnarled branch
arched by the weight of fruit, and one ripe peach
hangs a motionless inch from the gaping beak.

Here is transient beauty
caught in permanence;
but of what avail is such perpetual unattainment?

I know the stupid bird can never eat the stupid peach.

John Cremona

Children Playing

Children dance on the sands,
on the thin skin of evening, hands
scattering bats and shadows, feet
pressing the delayed, sweet
hours like harvested grapes
into the sheltered redness of
the centre of the earth.

Children drumming their mirth
in the face of a large sun falling
hopelessly into the sea.

Riding the moon like a white horse over
the static housetops and the charcoal trees.

The night is open on the world and breathes.

Peter Bland

Hawk and Rabbit

The hawk has turned, is treading air
Above a blue but lost horizon.
No sun, no other wings in sight,
No sun even—just the bare
Chill of infinity, and his eyes
Scything across the quiet fields.

Sleek in his innocence the rabbit lingers,
Tingling to stiffness, half aware
That time has already stopped. He nibbles
His green day back to comfort, stays his fear
Just long enough to let that far speck
Populate vacancy. There's a hint of breeze.

In between cold fur and burning feathers
A farmer drags the landscape by its heels.
Long furrows creep behind him but he leans
Into his future like a visionary—sees
Only the crisp curd of his passage curl
The earth aside. He hardly breathes.

Three lives! And clutching his whole life to him
The lingering rabbit outstays its scream,
The hawk hangs suspended by its eyes,
The farmer is the landscape he would be.

Gordon Challis

The Postman

This cargo of confessions, messages,
demands to pay, seems none of my concern;
you could say I'm a sort of go-between
for abstract agents trusting wheels will turn,
for censored voices stilled in space and time.

Some people stop me for a special letter;
one or two will tell me, if it's fine, that I
have picked the right job for this kind of weather.
A boy who understands life somewhat better
asks where postmen live—if not our office, why?

The work is quite routine but kindnesses
and awkward problems crop up now and then:
one old lady sometimes startles passers-by
claiming she is blameless as she hisses
at people present in her reminiscent ken;

she startled me as well the other day,
gave me a glass of lemonade and slipped
me a letter to deliver—'Don't you say
a word to anyone, it's no concern
of theirs, or yours.' Nor no more it was, except

here was this letter plainly marked 'To God'
and therefore insufficiently addressed.
I cannot stamp it now 'Return to sender'
for addressee and sender may be One. The best
thing is burn it, to a black rose He'll remember.

Charles Doyle

Massage with Gladiator Oil

For the whole man, well-rounded,
seek in Upper Queen Street.
Aided by thick jowled photographs
of fly-specked fellows, oiled
hair, white thighs, white torsos,
a card in a dust-clad window
conjures up miracles of
dumb-bells, trusses, biceps.

Hard by the Town Hall and
crouched across the street,
the muscularities
of the Methodist Mission,
the unguent is advertised.

Mind's food, also, is handy.
A few windows along (the flies
have got there, too) are displayed
paperbacks: *Love Me Forever,
She Laid It On The Line,*
and a sequel to *The Naked Lunch*
entitled *We Dress for Dinner.*

For the Pythagorean, opposite,
an array of electric guitars,
melodeons, ukeleles,
boxes of green felt picks,
curlicue saxophones.
Nearby the design begins
to shape, in the kindergarten
in a park where the sun
never ceases to shine.

One always hopes for
the classic transformation
to happen before one's eyes:
the skinny weed gingerly
tapping to be let in,
but standing back for the hero
to emerge trussed up in his muscles,
a dumb-bell bulging his biceps
—but it never happens. Waiting
in one's flabby flesh
one wonders if all this
build-up ends in dumbshows
on window-blinds; and cries
from one's heart to the unappearing
heroes, Rub down! Rub down!
Outside the lions roar.

Marilyn Duckworth

Child's Summer

This summer is the first that she will feel
In knees, throat, bone,
As something she could tame to be her own
To rub against her naked heel.

To purr across the vulnerable veins,
Rough lick the skin
Where childhood roughnesses have made it thin
And winter made it strange.

This summer is the first she will inhale
Pluming in nostrils sleek

As water in a duck's dim beak,
And a feathered tail.

Whittling into the kernel ear
Onto the stripped sense,
This summer crows for her in present tense,
A childhood chanticleer.

Kevin Ireland

Parade: Liberation Day

Think of a tree-lined city street
or an early autumn day;
fashion placards and bunting;
imagine a display
of dripping clothes
drying among the flags and signs
hung from the balconies;
think flags on to washing-lines.

People this street;
create language and breed.
Then think of—say—twenty tanks,
cornering at a terrifying speed,
powdering the paving-bricks;
imagine parachutes, drifting like thistle seed,
through the gusts of autumn leaves and sticks.

Now picture the infantry,
young, strong,
measuring with hob-nails
their heroic song.
Yet, make the song trail from the distance,
though the soldiers are near:
dreams must have music,
words must not be clear.

Think of a happy street
on an early autumn night;
imagine tables and chairs beneath the trees,
and the gay light
of coloured globes,
swaying with flag and sign.

People this street;
create chatter and wine.
Then think of—say—a billion stars,
and a moon darting with terrifying speed
from darkness, to darkness again.
Erase it all,
with sudden drenching rain.

Now picture the infantry,
cold, damp,
measuring with hob-nails
the way back to camp.
Yet, make this sound trail from the distance,
though the soldiers are near:
let them parade softly through dreamland,
their future is not clear.

Owen Leeming

Vespers

There is a bell behind the evening's bluishness
Whose harmonics tingle like hot little nerves.
The instant thickens and grows,
Damming back the future from the past,
Guarding over this Saturday, a moderate Westerly,
And no more strontium than usual, sport
For the sporting, melancholy, I think,
As this hour so often is, and yet laughs
Anticipatory, a swinging time ahead.
Like a compass
              the country seems to yaw
In an ocean of possibility, North Cape
Quavering an arc, so that all parts
Take on a queasy loosening of the status quo.
Who
      has heard the bell's true note,
The fundamental deep concussion of bronze? I,
I suspect all, have caught its overtones
Trembling outside the evening sky.
                        Why
Does this cool-stirring world feel as if fire
Is waiting around it, when we know there is space,
Only space, immoderately cold?

It is the hour
Of cold-meat meals, of the closing of bars,
Of showers and talcum.
The ink spreads through the sky.
The moment for spasm passes. Quite gently now,
What is to come drains into what has been,
The tremorous needle homes on North, and no one
Has had to worry. Only a cur's ear, mean,
Alert, instinctual, might catch the faint,
Continuing hum which shimmers from unearthly spires.

Gloria Rawlinson

Prologue on Alexander

After his feverish death in Babylon
memoirs were written, he was coined The Great;
his conquests were sung to rags, his name
was a gambit toppling kingdom and state.
After the practical honours had been done
dreamers flocked to his fame.

Whether or not he was born a fire from Zeus
('Not ichor, but mortal blood,' he said of his wounds),
we must concede his vision yielded ground
to worn-out troops chanting 'We want to go home'
in the Five River Country beyond the Hindu Kush.
The southerly kingdoms never heard his drum.

Fevered and drunk. Some baulked at the disgrace
of his death in Babylon where market coins
were stamped with his splendid face.
No one dared pursue his brave design
for the world-wide multi-racial State.
Praised be his strategy, his learning—not his vision.

Only the dreamers let their fancies fly:
King of the known earth he'd conquered the world—
and it was not enough. Grant him the sky.
Make him the Two Horned hero to be given
a giant eagle for mount, and be it believed
that Alexander had opened the vaults of Heaven.

Send the paragon down in a glass barrel
and grant him the deepest ocean to explore;

133

22,000 miles through years of peril
marching he dreamed of a conquered world—
let him reign over its future with no hidden shore
till his visions, and ours, are ruined or fulfilled.

Gloria Rawlinson

The Difference

A knife, now, for good or ill
snugly serves the hands of skill:
whittles a whistle, carves a name,
flies at a throw to the thrower's aim;
it slices ham, it skins a goat,
scrapes a carrot, or cuts a throat.
Your right hand marries some kind of knife
for better or worse the most of your life.

But a gun was fashioned for no other skill
and no other purpose than aiming to kill.

Max Richards

A Dip in the Gulf

To A.R., Poet

Back from our swim we sprawled about the room;
I balanced on the window ledge, and heard
within, music threading slow-spaced words;
outside, saw blue uniting clouds and men,
ships purposeful, yachts frivolous in the stream.
Birds reconciled with trees were stilled; within,
the music threaded amber beads of silence;
and pulsed in shadow, petal, was it?—moth?
moth, again beating; beating dark;
dark and speechless in the circling hand.

Extravagant, I thought how you surveyed
(instrument five-windowed, single-hearted)

such landmarks, seamarks, constellations as
fix beauty in a waste of hills, waves, days;
netted at least an inlet of experience;
how, without lying, braved the ocean silence.

The swimmer does not fear between the flags,
in earshot; and surface craft are surface craft:
a spot of trig, a trained eye, and you know
just where you are—bang in the middle of silence,
sinking, and does that chap know French?—you shouted
Au secours, Lord knows why; it seems he does—
he does the decent thing. . . . That belt he throws,
what strings attached? Oh, drowning men, we know,
will clutch at twigs, clouds that dissolve, moist petals.

Who's to say they are not saved? Why, you
and I, and drown together uncomplaining,
a moth or perfect shell encircled in the hand;
to amuse perhaps as curious amber (that
threaded, might tell a history of silence)
strollers by the Gulf, years hence, when ebbing tides
have drained the stream where men once sailed and drowned.

C. K. Stead

Four Minute Miler

None better knows what hunts us all
Around fixed circuits, in determined lanes,
The needle bearing down on those who fall,
The quick ones making gains.

Knows purpose too, the goal that moves
While we approach—as when a rail track sends
Its shafts ahead to meet like perfect loves
(Point never reached that lends

Grace to our dreams). For he will squeeze
The fractured seconds down till body burst;
Still the mechanic arm rides past, with ease
Breaking what hopes he nursed.

As well scholar, priest, king,
Eye fixed beyond, glory mounting behind,
All hunted man hunts with him the dear thing
He shall not find.

135

Robert Thompson

One Who Climbed Alone

Lacking apparent direction, or reference,
he who climbed alone, and had seen
rare among rocks the enamelled flower,
and wondered under the exploding sun,
stepped free from the engulfing scree
to discover the concealed pass—
saw safety in the incredible valley,
with upright smoke from simple chimneys,
terraced vineyards, orchards, and pastures,
the undisciplined gestures of children,
women washing clothes in a glacier stream,
and readily shed his city-made mask,
the passport, time would prove invalid,
his position in the psychopathic party;
grew happy, then, anonymous among dissenters
his world had hounded into happy exile.
No spies came from the other country.
only rumours of the capital, the search,
reached him, back-dated, from time to time—
had he lost his nerve, an accident?
or crossed the frontier? When questioned,
the surly guards were adamant, denying negligence.
Later, when others made the same journey,
braving the iron mountains, the spiteful guns,
many failed at first to recognise him,
the new love and freedom, conferring identity.

Raymond Ward

Settler and Stranger

Through the dark lens of our detachment, we
proceed to peer. Beyond the murmuring lips
and eyes flickering with animation,
beyond the brief society of sounds
they form with so much amiability,
beyond the heads and shoulders only, framed
like icons in the shimmering windows,
136 we stare into the night.

Across the harbour from their eminence
a constellation of interiors
like our own glitters impersonally.
We too would like to feel that we are known,
but with as little curiosity.
Hospitable though we first appear
to strangers, in them we soon lose interest
and stare into the night,

to where, against a clear and moonless sky,
the unfinished profile of the mountain
turns benignly from its own reflection.
What may, to some men once, have been a god
commanding sacrifice commands no more.
The myth extinct as a volcano, it
remembers chaos bubbling from the void
and stares into the night.

Out there the world, we know, is ill at ease.
As one can no longer be an island,
our role in these has yet to be defined
and, in our pantheon, the role of strangers:
which is to be impermanent, within
the most exclusive circles most alone,
to be, for us, a shade too near the bone.
We stare into the night.

Raymond Ward

For the Masked Ones

Here is a face for you, masked ones.
A real face with features on it.
The way it holds you in its glance
may startle, provoke brief disquiet;
yet there is nothing hostile here.
The forehead's active: as each thought
devises, it will subtly alter,
signal if it does not record.
Notice the eyes: enlarged, alert
one minute, deep-lidded the next.
Not glintings like glass by moonlight—
rich fires, each pupilled iris flecked
with gold. Responsive to the hour
and mood, see how they flare and fade.

137

Now, masked ones, look still lower.
Here is the nose. Not ruled quite straight
like yours, nor half so cardboard-stiff,
but mobile, hairy-nostrilled, pored;
of all features the most alive
once conscious, its owner expert.
The mouth, overshadowed almost,
curls just beneath. No mere dark slit
with lines for teeth, but with lips closed
or parted, flute-like, sensitive:
tight-squared in fury, roundly rolled
to hoot astonishment or kiss—
poised in this cup, the curving chin
which may lunge forward, lift with pride
or falter, scared from its position:
palpable, not blandly fitted.
A face. Not those weird things of yours,
pulped newspaper tied on with string.
All life's stigmata, lines and scars
afflict this naked, tender skin—
whatever its pigmentation,
brown, red or yellow, white or black.
Being itself it has no varnish on
which might obscure its light or dark
with aims or status, kinship, faith . . .
it needs no such apologies;
unlike you masked ones, likes to breathe
at liberty beneath all skies.
The face of neither beast nor god
nor demon: somewhat like your own
with your witch-doctor's headgear off
and superstitious rites outgrown.

J. E. Weir

Incident on a Country Road

I didn't stop, for it was only a house
caught in the hills' mist, and rain
was already breaking over the trees,
but I fancied I saw a face glance,
swift and white, from the shook curtains—
maybe I was wrong—it was that sort of day.

It was the kind of weather when trees were clouds
in a closed sky and the eye uncertain
in seeing. One couldn't be sure of fact
or fancy—projections of mist in the mind's
eye or cool-as-water reality.
Yet still, years later, there's one thing

that bothers me, though I've long since come
to the road's end. Who was it there
in the house caught in the hills' mist?
I'd give much to know. You see, somehow
I took the wrong turning, and only
that shape in the window can tell me where.

J. E. Weir

After the Rocket's Blast

*One day I dreamt about a cave, and a mountain blew up. The sea
caught alight, and everything started to be like war. . . .*
(The beginning of a child's essay.)

It may be the child was right.
Perhaps the sunstruck mountain
will melt and flow skyward
in mushroom dust, and no night
follow, while flaring seas fountain
and bubble after the rocket's blast.

Yet somehow you can't help feeling
the words said more than the child
could grasp; as if those desperate hours
meant fresh beginnings, men stealing
stunned from caves into the earth's wild
morning. (Why else did he draw flowers

and trees, vivid, at the page's ending?).

Patrick Wilson

The Abandoned Launch

Far from the summer crowds,
From the caravans
And surfing sands,
The campers' tents and cars,
The picnic spots,
Flag-flying yachts
And plying ferries, far
From the main shore she lies,
Hidden always
From summer's thousand eyes.

Far away,
Long lost, no one knows why,
Left secretly
To lie by a shallow sea
Ten feet above the tide,
On her small side.

Engine pulled out of her,
Useless, lying there
In disrepair,
Her shrivelled, paintless lines
Nude, narrow-shouldered,
And now half-mouldered,
The remnants of her bows
Still shows her curious name,
The Ant, to those who come
Upon her in her home.

No nearby tumbledown
Boatshed or tin shack
Comforts her wreck,
Showing upon the shore
Signs of ownership
Long since let slip.
No fence protects her beach,
No track leads up her hill
Affording still
140 Some earnest of goodwill.

Above her in the wind,
A peach tree on the hill
Blossoms at will
But no-one climbs to pick
Fruit hard and small,
Too plentiful:
An emblematic pair,
The launch and the wild tree,
Too fruitful he
In wasted fertility,

While she below him lies
In her quiet channel's head
Alone, unvisited
Save by some rare
Picnicker's boy
In clambering play.

Mark Young

The Quarrel

Put down those words,
rocks picked hastily from the beach of mind
for your defence. There is no need
for such an action
to be taken.

Unprime your anger. Cannons
never stopped a war but brought
more cannons in to bear. I
am unarmed. See, my hands
are empty.

If you must fight
then let it be with gestures. Once
stinging sentence tears my flesh
words cannot be
withdrawn.

Gestures can be bent
though, broken, turned from anger into love
by slightest twist of wrist.
Here is my hand:
please take it.

141

Mark Young

Grafton Bridge

Walking over the bridge, you cannot see
the immense baobab tree that the concrete
base resembles. Non-tropical in this
setting, its swollen bole sinks
into the gully, roots buried deep
amongst the oaks and onion flowers.

We live almost beneath it. The bridge
is our perpetual rainbow, monochrome
and monstrous, a sullen arch
that rises out of our lives
and rides above them. Yet it is not
intolerable. The quiet
that stems from it—the cars borne
far above our heads, the only exit
from the bottom of this street
a small damp path that dribbles down
into the gully—allows us to live
without its shadow clotting our existence.

All this to change, however, and is
already changing. The dull brass plaque
outside the old cemetery on the city side
honours the early settlers, is memory
of their deeds and 'dreams of progress'.
And 'progress' is what descendants also
dream about as they construct the motorway
that is erratically drawing nearer.
                              On the edge
of a condemned gully, we too await
the graders that will be our guillotines.

James A. Agboro

A Deserted Palm Tree

The weaver-birds have left you
Fretting like a giant ghost
Fleeing from a conjuror;
You that once held sway over
Your kindred;
Feared, honoured, flattered
And envied by all
For the endless revelry in your palace
As you welcomed new visitors
And bade farewell to old guests,
Amidst the flourishing of trumpets.

But now, only the withered fingers
Hanging loosely from your skeletal hands,
The thick bushy eyebrows which hide
Your wrinkled face,
And the feathers about you,
Are the only remains of your glorious past.

The gentlest wind that blows
Puts you in rage,
And makes you tell
Over and over again
The ingratitude of it all.

Minji Ateli

Superstition

I know
    that when a grumbling old woman
is the first thing I meet in the morning
    I must rush back to bed
    and cover my head.
That wandering sheep on a sultry afternoon
are really men come from their dark graves
    to walk in light
    in mortal sight.
That when my left hand or eyelid twitches
or when an owl hoots from a nearby tree
    I should need pluck—
    it means bad luck;

143

That drink spilled goes to ancestral spirits;
That witches dance in clumps of bananas;
That crumbs must be left in pots and plates
    until the morn
    for babes unborn.
That it's wrong to stand in doorways at dusk
for the ghosts must pass—they have right of way!
That when a hidden root trips me over
    fault's not in my foot;
    it's an evil root.
That if I sleep with feet towards the door
    I'll not long be fit.
    I know it—Yes, I know it!

John Pepper Clark

Abiku

Coming and going these several seasons,
Do stay out in the baobab tree,
Follow where you please your kindred spirits
If indoors is not enough for you.
True, it leaks through the thatch
When floods brim the banks
And the bats and the owls
Often tear in at night through the eaves,
And at harmattan, the bamboo walls
Are ready tinder for the fire
That dries the fresh fish up on the wrack.
Still, it's been the healthy stock
To several fingers, to many more will be
Who reach the sun.
No longer then bestride the threshold
But step in and stay
For good. We know the knife scars
Serrating down your back and front
Like beak of the sword-fish,
And both your ears, notched
As a bondsman to this house,
Are all relics of your first comings.
Then step in, oh step in and stay
For her body is tired,
Tired, her milk going sour
Where many more mouths gladden the heart.

John Pepper Clark
Night Rain

What time of night it is
I do not know
Except that like some fish,
Doped out of the deep,
I have bobbed up bellywise
From stream of sleep
And no cocks crow.
It is drumming hard here
And I suppose everywhere
Droning with insistent ardour upon
Our roof-thatch and shed
And through sheaves slit open
To lighting and rafters
I cannot make out overhead
Great water drops are dribbling,
Falling like orange or mango
Fruits showered forth in the wind,
Or perhaps I should say so
Much like beads I could in prayer tell
Them on string as they break
In wooden bowls and earthenware
Mother is busy now deploying
About our roomlet and floor.
Although it is so dark
I know her practised step as
She moves her bins, bags, and vats
Out of the run of water
That like ants filing out of the wood
Will scatter and gain possession
Of the floor. Do not tremble then
But turn, brothers, turn upon your side
Of the loosening mats
To where the others lie.
We have drunk tonight of a spell
Deeper than the owl's or bat's
That wet of wings may not fly.
Bedraggled upon the *iroko*,* they stand
Emptied of hearts, and
Therefore will not stir, no, not
Even at dawn for then
They must scurry in to hide.
So we'll roll over on our back

* (*iroko—tree associated with witches*)

And again roll to the beat
Of drumming all over the land
And under its ample soothing hand
Joined to that of the sea
We will settle to sleep of the innocent.

John Pepper Clark

Flight Across Africa

Earth, from miles up, lies
Slaughtered, the splintered green of plantain
About her. Still the coaches and trucks
Pummel the body, their tracks
Or scars, sharp lines against the skies,
Horizontal spits and stakes that pin
Down the calf. As shrine-attendant
Years back with others now initiate,
We stripped entrails, wet and warm, wide
Open in the streams. And the tide
Whichever way it came, took
Care of the mess and shook
Us all free. But those valleys and
Fields, showing ulcerated in the sun,
And highlands, so carved clean
The butchers no longer care to beat off
Flies, certainly are strange sacrifice
Not even this soap-sud sea we ride
Can flood. . . . And so the wild expectant take-off
Broke no bones, no banks, tho' it tore down
The bloody baft—which is enough touchdown.

Michael Echeruo

Prologue

(from *Poems to God and O'Brien*)

They turned their glances
    to the high roof;
    anxious with grimaces
    on their obvious faces;
    waiting for Angelus
    and candlelights
    in the stagnant summer heat.

Some sang aloud:
    'Save us, O save us
    from the jitters
    of our prime.'

And some others:
    'Hail! Alleluia!
    The doctors are gone;
    our sores shall fester
    in our hands till dawn,
    and the light of the sun
    shall shine us whole.'

We could hear other noises
    from the jukebox.

Then the celebrants turned pale
    with the dimmed lights;
    and so commenced the apocalypse
    of a sordid generation.

Romanus N. Egudu

These Merchants!

They carry our graves about
huntresses that hail in the haunt
as they hawk their wares,
no shrine is too sacred for their
fleshy feet, no room too ascetic

147

for its monastic odour
or study proof sufficient
for all its stacks, intellection
and logic against the scarlet lips
of the grinning vendors.

In this desert of juicy trees
those fall first and fast,
wealth and flesh and soul,
that most attain splendour,
iridescence of skin and limbs,
remorseless of nature mocked
and fulfilled at one straight blow
on a divan littered with decaying
leaves that yesterday were green
but today are here a spread
for fulfilment of loss.

The birds on the upper side of the shade
wobbling along both sides of a crescendo
in innocence which is ignorance
solemnise the repose of chaff taken for grain,
hurrying down the dips of their song
into the advertised vales
where the windows dressed
stand beyond the pale of reason.

Two quarters tip to tip of a moon
make a hollow whole,
and all within feel the centrifugal
pull that analyses the moon
for another synthesis.

Pol Nnamezie Ndu

The Last Trance

This last trance is the last dance,
the last dance of the children of the land
before several heroes of the land
to the pumping bloody abia beats
for a great thing is to come.

We assembled on a rainy morning;
dark, swampy, rainy morning

under the heavy-heavy storm
that carried away many red-eyed cocks
and they drowned, beating their wings against
    the raging storm,
beating, as if begging to us for help;
but we came, children of the land,
to see and hear the heroes of the land,
and dance the intoxicating abia beats
when the great day comes . . .

It has been long in coming, the great day,
with the merciless storm beating
and sweeping away many more cocks, and hens with them;

and the circle is formed,
the circle of the last dance,
with poets squatting in the circle-centre over tilted drums
to fire daubed chests, and tensed arms,
strained faces and bangled legs.

This last dance is a first trance,
for the limits of the floor are the limits of the skies
that merge into darkness, into oceans, into eternity
with the stars, the sun and the moon, which dance divided
over the floors
side by side with us,
children of the land.

We sail away in dance
till our floor takes a final plunge with the skies
and my voice blends with the end
which is only the trance of the dance;

long after the trance ascends
you will hear my solo blending with the abia beats,
shaking active hearts, soothing keen ears,
reddening fierce eyes . . .

Long after the trance ascends.

Gabriel Okara

The Mystic Drum

The mystic drum beat in my inside
and fishes danced in the rivers
and men and women danced on land
to the rhythm of my drum

But standing behind a tree
with leaves around her waist
she only smiled with a shake of her head.

Still my drum continued to beat,
rippling the air with quickened
tempo compelling the quick
and the dead to dance and sing
with their shadows—

But standing behind a tree
with leaves around her waist
she only smiled with a shake of her head.

Then the drum beat with the rhythm
of the things of the ground
and invoked the eye of the sky
the sun and the moon and the river gods—
and the trees began to dance,
the fishes turned men
and men turned fishes
and things stopped to grow—

But standing behind a tree
with leaves around her waist
she only smiled with a shake of her head.

And then the mystic drum
in my inside stopped to beat—
and men became men,
fishes became fishes
and trees, the sun and the moon
found their places, and the dead
went to the ground and things began to grow.

And behind the tree she stood
with roots sprouting from her
feet and leaves growing on her head
150   and smoke issuing from her nose

and her lips parted in her smile
turned cavity belching darkness.

Then, then I packed my mystic drum
and turned away; never more to beat so loud.

Gabriel Okara

Once Upon a Time

Once upon a time, son,
they used to laugh with their hearts
and laugh with their eyes;
but now they only laugh with their teeth,
while their ice-block-cold eyes
search behind my shadow.

There was a time indeed
they used to shake hands with their hearts;
but that's gone, son.
Now they shake hands without hearts
while their left hands search
my empty pockets.

'Feel at home,' 'Come again,'
they say, and when I come
again and feel
at home, once, twice,
there will be no thrice—
for then I find doors shut on me.

So I have learned many things, son.
I have learned to wear many faces
like dresses—homeface,
officeface, streetface, hostface, cock-
tailface, with all their conforming smiles
like a fixed portrait smile.

And I have learned too
to laugh with only my teeth
and shake hands without my heart.
I have also learned to say, 'Goodbye'
when I mean 'Goodriddance';
to say 'Glad to meet you,'
without being glad; and to say 'It's been
nice talking to you,' after being bored.

151

But believe me, son.
I want to be what I used to be
when I was like you. I want
to unlearn all these muting things.
Most of all, I want to relearn
how to laugh, for my laugh in the mirror
shows only my teeth like a snake's bare fangs!

So show me, son,
how to laugh; show me how
I used to laugh and smile
once upon a time when I was like you.

Gabriel Okara

One Night at Victoria Beach

The wind comes rushing from the sea,
the waves, curling like mambas, strike
the sands and recoiling hiss in rage
washing the Aladuras' feet pressing hard
on the sand and with eyes fixed hard
on what only hearts can see, they shouting
pray, the Aladuras pray; and coming
from booths behind, compelling highlife
forces ears; and car lights startle pairs
arm in arm passing washer-words back
and forth like haggling sellers and buyers—

Still they pray, the Aladuras pray
with hands pressed against their hearts
and their white robes pressed against
their bodies by the wind; and drinking
palm-wine and beer, the people boast
at bars at the beach. Still they pray.

They pray, the Aladuras pray
to what only hearts can see while dead
fishermen long dead with bones rolling
nibbled clean by nibbling fishes, follow
four dead cowries shining like stars
into deep sea where fishes sit in judgement;

and living fishermen in dark huts
sit around dim lights with Babalawo
throwing their souls in four cowries
on sand, trying to see tomorrow.

Still, they pray, the Aladuras pray
to what only hearts can see behind
the curling waves and the sea, the stars
and the subduing unanimity of the sky
and their white bones beneath the sand.

And standing dead on dead sands,
I felt my knees touch living sands—
but the rushing wind killed the budding words.

C. Uche Okeke

They Walked and Talked

They talked and walked,
walked and talked and talked—
talkative homing dames;
mothers, grandmothers, all homing,
returning from a distant mart
baskets on heads, words on lips—
gossip or tall tales of folk at home.

They clapped their hands;
they screamed from time to time;
they moved their hands in most expressive ways—
their hands spoke even louder than their tongues—
as they swept like a great Saharan wind
along the winding beaten tracks
before them, silent, deserted.

Not even the discordant croaking of the toad,
not even the noise of insects here and there,
not even the songs of birds everywhere,
were heard above the noise of these homing folk
who (forgetful of the ancient saying
that even blades of grass are living ears)
could not restrain their long and wagging tongues.

Christopher Okigbo

From: *Distances*

I
FROM FLESH into phantom on the horizontal stone:
I was the sole witness to my homecoming . . .

Serene lights on the other balcony:
redolent fountains bristling with signs—

But what does my divine rejoicing hold?
A bowl of incense, a nest of fireflies?

I was the sole witness to my homecoming . . .

For in the inflorescence of the white
chamber, a voice, from very far away,
chanted, and the chamber descanted, the birthday of earth,
paddled me home through some dark
labyrinth, from laughter to the dream.

Miner into my solitude,
incarnate voice of the dream,
you will go,
with me as your chief acolyte,
again into the ant-hill . . .

I was the sole witness to my homecoming . . .

II
DEATH LAY in ambush that evening in that island;
voice sought its echo that evening in that island.

And the eye lost its light,
the light lost its shadow.

For the wind, eternal suitor of dead leaves,
unrolled his bandages to the finest swimmer . . .

It was an evening without flesh or skeleton;
an evening with no silver bells to its tale;
without lanterns, evening without buntings;
and it was an evening without age or memory—

for we are talking of such commonplaces,
and on the brink of such great events . . .

And in the freezing tuberoses of the white
chamber, eyes that had lost their animal
colour, havoc of eyes of incandescent rays,
pinned me, cold, to the marble stretcher,

until my eyes lost their blood
and the blood lost its odour,

and the everlasting fire from the oblong window
forgot the taste of ash in the air's marrow:

anguish and solitude . . .
Smothered, my scattered
cry, the dancers,
lost among their own
snares; the faces,
the hands held captive;
the interspaces
reddening with blood;

and behind them all,
in smock of white cotton,
Death herself,
the chief celebrant,
in a cloud of incense,
paring her fingernails . . .

At her feet rolled their heads like cut fruits;
about her fell
their severed members, numerous as locusts.

Like split wood left to dry, the dismembered
joints of the ministrants piled high.

She bathed her knees in the blood of attendants;
her smock in entrails of ministrants . . .

III
VI
THE SEASON the season
in tall woods in clearings;
the season the season
on stone steps, the dream . . .

Come into my cavern,
Shake the mildew from your hair;
Let your ear listen:
My mouth calls from a cavern . . .

Lo, it is the same blood that flows . . .

155

Shadows distances labyrinths violences,
Skeletal oblong
of my sentient being, I receive you
in my perforated
mouth of a stranger, empty of meaning,
like stones without juice—

the goat still knows its fodder
from leopards on its trail—

For it is the same blood,
through the same orifices,
the same branches
trembling intertwined,
and the same faces
in the interspaces.

And it is the same breath, liquid, without acolyte,
like invisible mushrooms on the stones' surfaces.

And at this chaste instant of delineated anguish,
the same voice, importunate, aglow with the goddess—

unquenchable, yellow, darkening homeward
like a cry of wolf above crumbling houses—

strips the dream naked,
bares the entrails;

and in the orangery of immense corridors,
I wash my feet in your pure head, O maid,

and walk along your feverish, solitary shores,

seeking, among your variegated teeth,
the tuberose of my putrescent laughter:

I have fed out of the drum
I have drunk out of the cymbal

I have entered your bridal
chamber; and lo,

I am the sole witness to my homecoming.

Note: *Distances* is the fifth part of a much longer work entitled
Labyrinths, and was written just after Christopher Okigbo under-
went surgery under general anaesthesia. 'In *Distances,*' the poet
says, 'the poet-hero undergoes a total liberation from all mental,

emotional and psychic tension through sensual anaesthesia; and
the self that suffers, that experiences, becomes sublimated to the
supreme spirit that wounds, that nurtures all creation.'
Christopher Okigbo is thought to have been killed in October, 1967 whilst
serving with the Biafran Army in the Nigerian Civil War.

Edward C. Okwu

Confession

Like a mischievous boy,
I peep through the door-hole,
beholding a naked old man, half asleep,
spent,
on the bamboo bed;

and I raise a fire alarm,
false,
for the man to scuttle away
to his shrine, his *ikenga*, his life-wire, his soul,
into the cold claws of the harmattan;

while I,
showing broken teeth of laughter,
sneak into his hut
to emerge later with large rounded yams,
hurriedly treading on scattered corns,
mouth bursting with red-ripe nuts
and eyes squinting
sentinel-wise
like a mischievous boy.

Mabel Imoukhuede Segun

The Pigeon-Hole

How I wish I could pigeon-hole myself
and neatly fix a label on!
But self-knowledge comes too late
and by the time I've known myself
I am no longer what I was.

I knew a woman once
who had a delinquent child.

she never had a moment's peace of mind
waiting in constant fear,
listening for the dreaded knock
and the cold tones of a policeman:
'Madam, you're wanted at the station.'
I don't know if the knock ever came
but she feared on right until
we moved away from the street.
She used to say,
'It's the uncertainty that worries me—
if only I knew for certain . . .'

If only I knew for certain
what my delinquent self would do . . .
But I never know
until the deed is done
and I live on fearing,
wondering which part of me will be supreme—
the old and tested one, the present
or the future unknown.
Sometimes all three have equal power
and then
I long for a pigeon-hole.

Wole Soyinka

Death in the Dawn

Traveller, you must set out
At dawn. And wipe your feet upon
The dog-nose wetness of earth.

Let sunrise quench your lamps, and watch
Faint brush pricklings in the sky light
Cottoned feet to break the early earthworm
On the hoe. Here shadows stretch with sap
Not twilight's death and sad prostration.
This soft kindling, soft receding breeds
Racing joys and apprehensions for
A naked day. Burdened hulks retract,
Steep to the mist in faceless throng
To wake the silent markets—swift, mute
Processions on grey byways. . . .

On this

Counterpane, it was—

Sudden winter at the death
Of dawn's lone trumpeter. Cascades
Of white feather-flakes, but it proved
A futile rite. Propitiation sped
Grimly on, before.

> The right foot for joy, the left, dread
> And the mother prayed, Child
> May you never walk
> When the road waits, famished.

Traveller you must set forth
At dawn
I promise marvels of the holy hour
Presages as the white cock's flapped
Perverse impalement—as who would dare
The wrathful wings of man's Progression. . . .

But such another Wraith! Brother,
Silenced in the startled hug of
Your invention—is this mocked grimace
This closed contortion—I?

Okogbule Wonodi

*Ekwe Eme**

My arrows,
   like the village boys',
   are far spent
   in aimless shots at lizards
   while squirrels and weaverbirds
   harvest the fruits on the farms
   and hornbills and eagles
   perch at arm's length . . .

But I have farms to guard
   and game to shoot,
   and these arrows
   that I now make,
   new and fangled,
   shall make meat of birds
   and leave the farm fruitful.

---

* *Ekwe Eme, an Ibo expression which means saying something and being able to achieve it. Often used to describe a 'go-getter'.*

Zulfikar Ghose

Abbaye de Sénanque

On the hilltop at Gordes, commandingly
surveying a valley, are the houses
of an abandoned village: the outward
civilized structure contains emptiness.

Nearby, the road furtively descends to
a forested valley: almost submerged
among pines, wild olives and oaks, is an
abbey where monks still live an ordered life.

Who regards exposure as liberty?
Obscure among the pines, insects are free.
While the monks at Sénanque sell liqueur,
wind and sun call at the houses at Gordes.

Zulfikar Ghose

Jets from Orange

Jets from Orange, low above Mont Ventoux,
dive into valleys of vineyards and rise
over forested hills: an ostentatious exercise
of the skill and endurance of the crew.

This is olive-growing country, Provence,
whose strips of farms are runways for the sun's
landings. Other more ancient disciplines
than aerodynamics control the plants.

The jets fly over and return to base.
They cannot revoke the earth's accession to the sun
whether they come from beyond the mountain
or from beyond the ocean or from outer space.

M. K. Hameed

Street Scene

There's no running and escape
From the torrent of moonlight;
It's the disconsolate time when
Greatness is all gone out
Of the big bright day,
And silence is sampled softness
Of relief and resurgence
For a very new beginning:
An expert start of a search
For a priceless pearl concealed
Within the crusty corner of cold bread.

Torments and all distress
Lie trellised in caged patterns
On the cool moonwashed courtyard;
The aroma of smoke sits in repose
Beneath curtainless doorways,
And the miasma of sweaty existence
Rises like the apparition of
Fables far-fetched and
Some serious myths of unconcern
Stored in empty tin cans;
And the silver leaves of moonlight
Skidding on the silent rooftops
Nag the sleeping shades, nestling
In houseful streets bursting at the seams.

Adrian Husain

That Cold Land

Rivers, icicles, rocks. That cold
land has left me somewhat
prone to lavish mournfulness.

And those snows, whose nullity
bereft me of the ribald pose of yesterday,
have made me

161

somehow nude and featureless,
uncertain of the postures life would like me to assume.
Therefore grief is

my excuse for not remembering
how, or whether I was happy.
I never thought re-birth

would be like this, a kind of
exposure of the guilty glands,
which are, however, dead.

To all those cool, untainted souls,
to plants and trees, the vagrant rose,
whose secret is that

they have no secrets,
and thus are silent in the telling—
my voice is

the knower's curse, and cannot
—their breezes tell them—
cannot ever climb to ecstasy.

Taufiq Rafat

The Time to Love

The time to love
is when the heart says so.

Who cares
    if it is muddy august
    or tepid april?—
for Love's infallible feet
    step daintily
    from vantage to vantage
    to the waiting salt-lick.

If Spring
has any significance,
it is for us,
 the rhymesters,
 who need
 a bough to perch on
 while we sing.

Love is a country
with its own climate.

Taufiq Rafat

After the Whimpering

After the whimpering now
Time for full-throated song;
The joy and abandon
Such as rude boys know.

Time for a word of nonsense
Again. So let mad eyes
Sparkle, while behind them
The sorrows sleep like swans.

N. M. Rashed

The Smell of Mankind

From where has this smell of Man suddenly come?
Jungle demons stand stone-still;
Their footprints turn to fetters on their feet;
The smell of Man.
In dim jungle meadows,
In the moonlight, they dance without fear,
 without sorrow.
But now, their feet are numb, their hands cold,
Their eyes petrified, without light.
A single whiff has turned them white with fear;

163

For them, one smell is enough.
Who is a match for them?
A shadow, hidden in the Tree of Time, among the
    branches of months and years,
Looks on them through tangled silent branches.
One smell of Him and they panic.
They turn to wax.
Yes; tonight Man will descend,
And demons' valour will be shattered.

(Translated from the Urdu by
M. H. K. Qureshi and Carlo Coppola)

Phillippa Berlyn

Balancing Rocks

These old rocks
are wise with wonders seen,
where the sleek leopard rules
his kingdom rust and grey
and fringed with green.

Accusing fingers, raised
to a rock-free heaven,
gargoyles in stone
and lichen,
secrets locked in granite,
mountains poised on pebbles,
they stand these rocks
as evidence
of where the earth once trembled.

Now old dogface the baboon,
blue-bottomed and grotesque,
plays round their confines.
He is the parody of man,
running his pack,
quarrelling, lecherous,
barking at the moon
where it hangs like a blood drop
from the sky.

So natural, so like a man he acts
that there is room for questioning
which is the parody, what are the facts?

Noëline Barry

Living Water

The Bantu maiden came to draw
Her brimming bucket from the well,
She covered it with leaves. I saw
That no drop fell.

She raised it proudly to her head;
I watched the water rock and swell,
But as she passed, with buoyant tread,
Not one drop fell.

I lift my brimming cup of love
In salutation to the sun,
And though I spill it all the way,
I shall lose none.

Gaston Bart-Williams

god bless U S

dreaming
I saw a butterfly in the night
yellow bright and beautiful
I watched you call it red and watched you crush it
and all I did was to get up
and wash my face

awake
I listen to old jazz
soul jazz
and dig the strokes
the sharp edge of the penetrating steel
awake
I listen to same home steel
digging through Vietcongs
and all I did was to get up
and wash my face

watching
you soul brother
having heard your wail in Mississippi
watching you rot in mother Harlem
noting your bullets whizzing through your yellow brother
and the tattoo on your heroic skin
god bless U S
I might as well get up again
and wash my eyes and ears

Gaston Bart-Williams

Omega

Wash
your scalpels
with
my tears of joy
then
reach out for
my heart and
dig!

I bleed not
but
oh how much I
wish
that the songs of
my solitude
will
lull you to
slumber
in my place.

Gaston Bart-Williams

Despondence Blues

All night long Lord
'ave been waitin' for your call
All night long Lord
'ave been lookin' for your hand
If you don't come and take me Lord
Them folks will crush me up
If you don't come and take me Lord
Them folks will crush me down

All night long Lord
'ave been searchin' for your face
Searchin' and searchin' Lord
Searchin' for your face
But all I find aroun' me
Are chains and locks and bars
All I find aroun' me Lord
Are chains and locks and bars

Fence and walls aroun' me
Chains aroun' my feet
I search for a freedom picture
I search for a smilin' face
But all I get for searchin'
Are blows and kicks and wounds
All I get for searchin' Lord
Are wounds and wounds and wounds

Come down here my Lord
Come here and set me free
168   I know you are not blind Lord

And I know you are not deaf
'ave been praying and crying Lord
And I know that you're alive somewhere
If you don't come and free me Lord
Do you know what am gonna do

Am gonna paint your picture
The picture of your loving grace
A picture of a hangman the picture of his ghost
A picture of a horror monster with a hard and cruel face
If you don't come and free me Lord
That's jus' what am gonna do
If you don't come and free me
That's jus' what am gonna do

Delphine King

The Child

When will this child be black?
When will the child in ebony be carved
Who occupies a place conspicuous there
Where all our guests arrive?
Who greets them first? A child!
A child that calmly pours
Out of a bowl into the fountain pure
The flowing liquid.
But behold the child is white.

The image of conditioned minds
Unwitting, unsuspectingly exposed
In the figure of a child
To all the world who look to us
For inspiration, leadership.
When will the child in ebony carved,
When will the child be black?

Abioseh Nicol

The Meaning of Africa

Africa, you were once just a name to me
But now you lie before me with sombre green challenge
To that loud faith for freedom (life more abundant)
Which we once professed shouting
Into the silent listening microphone
Or on an alien platform to a sea
Of white perplexed faces troubled
With secret Imperial guilt; shouting
Of you with a vision euphemistic
As you always appear
To your lonely sons on distant shores.

Then the cold sky and continent would disappear
In a grey mental mist.
And in its stead the hibiscus blooms in shameless scarlet
and the bougainvillea in mauve passion
entwines itself around strong branches
the palm trees stand like tall proud moral women
shaking their plaited locks against the
cool suggestive evening breeze;
the short twilight passes;
the white full moon turns its round gladness
towards the swept open space
between the trees; there will be
dancing tonight; and in my brimming heart
plenty of love and laughter.
Oh, I got tired of the cold northern sun
Of white anxious ghost-like faces
Of crouching over heatless fires
In my lonely bedroom.
The only thing I never tired of
was the persistent kindness
Of you too few unafraid
Of my grave dusky strangeness.

So I came back
Sailing down the Guinea Coast.
Loving the sophistication
Of your brave new cities:
Dakar, Accra, Cotonou,
Lagos, Bathurst and Bissau;
Liberia, Freetown, Libreville,
Freedom is really in the mind.

Go up-country, so they said,
To see the real Africa.
For whomsoever you may be,
That is where you come from.
Go for bush, inside the bush,
You will find your hidden heart,
Your mute ancestral spirit.
And so I went, dancing on my way.

Now you lie before me passive
With your unanswering green challenge.
Is this all you are?
This long uneven red road, this occasional succession
Of huddled heaps, of four mud walls
And thatched, falling grass roofs
Sometimes ennobled by a thin layer
Of white plaster, and covered with thin
Slanting corrugated zinc.
These patient faces on weather-beaten bodies
Bowing under heavy market loads.
The pedalling cyclist wavers by
On the wrong side of the road,
As if uncertain of his new emancipation.
The squawking chickens, the pregnant she-goats
Lumber awkwardly with fear across the road,
Across the windscreen view of my four-cylinder kit car.
An overladen lorry speeds madly towards me
Full of produce, passengers, with driver leaning
Out into the swirling dust to pilot his
Swinging obsessed vehicle along.
Beside him on the raised seat his first-class
Passenger, clutching and timid; but he drives on
At so, so many miles per hour, peering out with
Bloodshot eyes, unshaved face and dedicated look;
His motto painted on each side: Sunshine Transport,
We get you there quick, quick. The Lord is my Shepherd.

The red dust settles down on the green leaves.
I know you will not make me want, Lord,
Though I have reddened your green pastures
It is only because I have wanted so much
That I have always been found wanting.
From South and East, and from my West
(The sandy desert holds the North)
We look across a vast continent
And blindly call it ours.
You are not a country, Africa,
You are a concept,
Fashioned in our minds, each to each,

To hide our separate fears,
To dream our separate dreams.
Only those within you who know
Their circumscribed plot,
And till it well with steady plough
Can from that harvest then look up
To the vast blue inside
Of the enamelled bowl of sky
Which covers you and say
'This is my Africa' meaning
'I am content and happy.
I am fulfilled, within,
Without and roundabout
I have gained the little longings
Of my hands, my loins, my heart
And the soul that follows in my shadow.'
I know now that is what you are, Africa:
Happiness, contentment, and fulfilment,
And a small bird singing on a mango tree.

Mazisi Kunene

To the Proud

In the twirling mountains overhung with mist
Foretell Nodongo the proud name of the subsequent hours
Since, when you beat the loud music of your wings,
The secret night creeps underneath the measured time.

When you behold the fixed bulk of the sun
Jubilant in its uncertain festivals
Know that the symbol on which you stand shall vanish
Now that the dawning awaits us with her illusions.

Assemble the little hum of your pealing boast
For the sake of the reward meted to Somndeni
Who sat abundantly pride-flowing
Till the passer-by vultures of heaven overtook him.

We who stood by you poverty-stricken
Shall abandon you to the insanity of licence
And follow the winding path
Where the wisdom granaries hold increase.

Then shall your nakedness show
Teasing you before the unashamed sun.
Itching you shall unfurl the night
But we the sons of Time shall be our parents' race.

Laurence Lerner

'I Want You to Wake'

I lay asleep in the grass all afternoon
Smothered in sunshine, hardly hearing the cars,
The dogs or the lawnmowers coughing; only my son
Clambered over my limbs and beat at my ears.
'Why are you lying asleep
I want you to read my book
I want you to kick my ball, to buy a cake
I want you to go to the shop and buy a cake
I want you to go to the shop and buy a sweet
Why are you lying such a long time why?'

Sleeping I reach a hand
To fondle the empty afternoon; the air
Bristles with birdsong, and the sharp caress

173

Of the nagging grasses rubs my resentful flesh.
Clusters of paws on my neck
Suddenly patter and tear
The wrappings of sleep and complicate my hair.

'Why do you tell the cat to go away
Daddy why do you fall asleep all day
Daddy Daddy why do people sleep
How long goes past before they all wake up
I want you to read my book I want you to wake.'

You want me to wake, and I wake. You know I will do
(In the end) whatever you want—read, spend or play,
Or lie on the grass while you climb on my limbs or twist
My words and my hair.
   And when what you want is that you
And not I should be left alone,
That the smothering sun
Should crush my sweet flesh in the grass; that I sleep
 and sleep
All day and never get up,
  I will do that too.

David Wright

Grasmere Sonnets

I

In a tea-garden overhanging Rotha
On whose clear surface cardboard packages
And other discards take their voyages
To the quiet lake, I wondered what he'd say,
Old mountain-trotter with a nose like Skiddaw,
Safely asleep there where the river nudges
Its coco-cola can into the sedges,
Were his bleak eye to brood upon our day.

Exultant at the goings-on of nature,
Eavesdropping winds' and waters' talk,
That tough egoist, bathetic as ever,
Overlooks from Town-end a macadam car-park,
Folkweave booths, postcards, and suburbia,
The desert of our century; he'll not baulk.

II

He was always fortunate and was given
An enviable present; which he employed

174

To provide the inanimate with a voice,
A mountain stream giving a tongue to a mountain.
For he said that they haunted him like passion,
The air, earth, and water, and light and clouds,
With which he would intelligibly rejoice,
At one with their solitary interaction.

But his present is past and has for audience
A torn paper floating on the water,
A smell of tar and coaches; a technological present
Of bodily comfort and abominable fear,
Of no resolution and no independence;
Yet never think he is not with us here.

III

The mountain winds pummel Fairfield and Helvellyn
Scrubbing the hills with a blanket of vapour.
Recognise there the inimical nature
Of those elements beyond our controlling
If any are. Call it a foretelling
Of our victorious and rational slaughter
Of useless creation: his versing nostalgia
For the other lives that we see disappearing.

Let him lie there by Rotha without remark;
Hiding and half disclosing, the veils of rain
Make a chinese painting of his ashen lake,
Of the slopes where woods deciduously mourn
Another autumn about to overtake
A summer's progress with a bony arm.

IV

There is a cragbound solitary quarter,
Hawk's kingdom once, a pass with a tarn
High on its shoulder; inscribed on a stone
With graveyard letters, a verse to his brother*
Says it was here they parted from each other
Where the long difficult track winding down
A bald blank bowl of the hills may be seen
Leading the eye to a distant gleam of water.

After that last goodbye and shake of the hand
A bright imagination flashed and ended;
The one would live on, for forty years becalmed
Among the presences he had commanded,
Those energies in which the other foundered,
Devoured by wind and sea in sight of land.

* *John Wordsworth, Master of the* Earl of Abergavenny, *wrecked off the Dorset coast, 1805.*

S. A. El-Miskery

The Crack

Crack the glass,
and the crack
will always remain.
The human heart
has the same vein;
it's just as delicate
to the strain.

Once it is hurt,
it is too hard
to fade the stain.
Though parts can
be fixed together,
you've just to touch the wound
to make it drain again.

Kanti Chandra Garg

Will You Come

Will you come and row with me
In my boat in the moonlight?
Come and hear the stars with me,
As they sing in the milky night.
For you dark peacocks cry,
And the wide-eyed lilies are still
As they glide on the mirror water.
Reeds part as we slip between;
A dog yelps once and is gone,
And the night is ours.

Yusuf O. Kassam

The Recurrent Design

The sun set, night came, and everything was dark—
The signal to stir.

Out in the rough sea the propellers churned
And the bewildered rudder trailed behind;
Shovels dug the ground mile after mile;
Heavy rubber smouldered on lonely roads;
Chains of steel plate crushed the plants and the stones,
While a droning echo filled the pierced sky.

Soon the sea, the land, and the sky were quiet;
The sweat was wiped and the pistons rested,
And all movement ceased.

Then came the long and nervous waiting:
The clock ticked,
The heart beat,
The sentry stepped,
The eyes gleamed,
And the morse peeped under a cold finger.

At dawn the clock pointed the hour, and
'Strike!' shrilled the sharp calculated command.
At once the fever and the frenzy mushroomed,
While the rising sun splashed red everywhere:
    Those who were beginning to waken
    Never awoke again.

Rose Mbowa

Ruin

Up on a hill it stood immovable,
Dark and gloomy in the dusk;
A heavy silence hung in the air
Restraining her courage, her will;
But on she walked.

A cricket whistled, breaking the silence,
Lighting her path and her will;
Then suddenly it stopped,
As if suppressed by a heavy hand,
Still . . . on she moved.

Every move drew her nearer,
Every move gravitated towards the gloom;
Giant trees, heavy and dark before her rose,
Guards on duty, erect in the dark,
Through them she pushed.

With eyes closed, arms outstretched,
She groped in an envelope of black;
The air grew dense and doomed,
Her heart drummed faster and louder;
To the door she stepped.

With trembling hands she pushed,
A squeal pierced the air;
Flashes blinded her sight;
And down she descended at a blow,
On the grim rude stone.

John Nagenda

Flutes and Indians

always the flute-thin trembling
of the music of sadness
trembles and flutes
in the core of myself
beneath the laughter and the noise

now here in albuquerque
new mexico usa
with the closeness and the heat
there is the piped sound of
a flute alone
of a nature strange and
i suppose therefore indian

outside the land is
brown and bare and cries
of indians dead and gone
but as reminders their blankets are here
and wherever i turn i see their names

who sings songs of the warriors dead
who tickles laughter from the sides of rocks

and here walk the conquerors
as the music stops

John M. Ruganda

Victory?

Age, cruel age, river of wrought havoc,
Clutches at my crumbling frame
In a breath-bankrupt pothole—
A defeat imposed in a moment of victory.

My river meanders to the hungry sea
Like an impatient sprinter
Who bolts away before the signal,
And slips when the gun is fired.

I have farmed in the pene-plain,
Mined in the ungraded profile,
Strolled in the green-shodden delta
And marked the lovers' course,
But with untraceable footprints.

Now, a weather-beaten vagabond, I pant abysswards,
like a one-sonned mother duelling with his parting life,
Or like a haphazardly tumbling stone, without moss,
—No, with the moss drifting away
Over the steaming cataract yonder.

Proscovia Rwakyaka

The Inmates

Now when into the far past I pry
With a sharp but puzzled mind
I remember vaguely;
A young girl among towering maize;
Her short uncertain fingers
Pressing one, another
And then another . . .
But where was this field so large?

I remember a large large building
Youngsters resounding,
Twinkles, giggles and tears,
Lost playmates
Now wavering like a dying flame.
Will I ever re-trace?
Still far in the past
Faded images will linger.

I remember calm evenings:
A band tamed and captured
By rumbling wonders
Of mighty elephant, witty hare,
Dashing lads and pretty girls.
These readily return:
Not the faces and the voices
Creeping farther and farther.

John B. K. Ssemuwanga

Dual Piety

Somewhere in the distance church bells are chiming,
Chiming and beckoning me to the abode of
    sacred mysteries,
Mysteries reverently guarded by cold holy walls;
And my servile soul harks to the angelic melody
And flaps wing and flies thither.

It is Sunday morning, and the bells seem to toll
The ebb of ancestral piety,
Piety dinned by Christian chime
And tarnished by rituals ministered by infallible arrivals,

Yet defying latinized devotion
And yearning to woo wayward generations back to
    time's old rites;
And my cleft soul listens to the potent words of the gods.

Thus my confused self floats to the two temples
And reveres the God of gods
And communes with the gods of old.

I pose before the candled God
And scent the blessing of the blessed incense,
And listen to the words of holy stories,
Stories read from sacred scribes.
And surfeited with heavenly faith I swoon
And crumble down in prostrate adoration.

Yet my sceptical self wanders from hither
And sits with recusant worshippers
And sings the songs of awe
And throbs to the rhythm of reverent music
And bathes in the blood of the white goat,
And seems to sigh—
Oh gods, gods, we are lost.

And in dual piety I cry out to God
To water the plains
And the gods whisper: it will rain.

Tejani

Night Illusion

Coming by last night
we were charmed by
silvery moonlight over
vast green tea fields.
The road was a ribbon
of white in the darker shade
of the tea fields.

Round the bend lay a
small hillock, rounded
and soft like a man's buttock.
It slept there so quietly.
We must come and see it
again tomorrow.

The next morning, the purring of the
car's engine was harsh.
It disturbed the stillness around.
The road now was sandy and hard
in the glare of the sun
and seemed to disturb
the great green tea fields.

Round the bend lay our hillock.
But look! Who has wrenched
my heart and made me
stand still?
A great grey gash has been
torn in the side of the hill
as if a lion had sunk its
gory teeth in the soft human
flesh and torn a large chunk out.
Bald and uglily grinning
it stands, helpless, like an
old grey man with a toothless face.
This is the sand pit for
the tea factory over there.

The emerald of the grass shines
and stretches
but cannot hide the
man-made nakedness of its
side.

Timothy Wangusa

A Strange Wind

A strange wind is blowing, dust fills our eyes;
we turn and walk the unintended way.
We press our sore eyes and re-open them
to expanded horizons, to a new day.
The narrow circle of our cherished experience breaks,
our trusted gods dissolve and ghosts vanish,
disembodied voices announce the world news—
we see the hidden side of the moon;
the dead man's eye transfers to the living;
the atom splits and the nightingale croaks;
economics opposes charity,
law protects wizards and forbids justice;
the small nation shouts, and the big one brags;
futile raids cease, and global wars commence;
and the rude son strikes the father. . . .

A. Alvarez
The Hunt

The air is dry as salt, the desert ribbed
Between scrub and heat and mountain.
The sun bakes like an eye in a blank face,
Or, delicate as a mother, swells the moon.

By night the stars are touchable as fruit
About the hut; the undergrowth is quick
With hidden life. Deer tread the cooling fields
Like ghosts, and shrill as ghosts the swaying bats.

And so I hunt by night. I see with my feet
Among the piñon, along vague, struggling tracks
Up from the cabin, through the breathing forest,
Moving by moonlight. Silent. Silence. Stealth.

A tentative sound begins: a woman talking
Raptly, excitedly murmuring to herself?
The mountain stream runs thin as breath through its shallows.
I follow the woman's voice to its dammed-up source

Where logs are tangled thick and silt builds up,
Where water flickers fragile and loose as light
And something hesitates: a shadow drinks at the clearness,
Insubstantial, takes substance like food from a cup.

I gather, silent and poised among the bushes.
(Life of my life, flesh of my flesh) I aim
And (with my body I thee worship) fire.
The creature rises, arches, flays the pool,

Its legs as taut as needles, its head wild.
It leaps like a cry on the air, is torn inside
And gives out its life to the watery silt and the moon.
Shapeless. Jerking. Loveless. Without pride.

Slowly the noise dies away. The heart's crashing
Fades up the mountain and settles, too, the shocked
Whisper and rustle of beasts who have seen the slaying.
The creature trembles. It is my own blood spurts.

Alison Bielski

Twentieth Century Flood

I

When the rain started to fall, it was Wednesday,
middle of the week, a cold Spring noon
heavily breathing dampness of early March.
Then it began. Clouds swelled, exploded,
threw down rivers of rain. It dented pavements
with iron drops, heavy, terrible.
We drew curtains, lit lamps, but still we heard
rain, rain, rain, and so it continued to fall, drum
down its evil clatter, beat on anvils
of town, steel city, highway and springing forest.
Continents shivered and shrank, as the storm
hammered the startled earth to forge a mighty flood.

It went on for days, a week, two, a month of rain,
and still and still and still it fell.
We saw death's face in rivers, grinning in giant
torrents: abandoning houses
we dared not turn where wishes, achievements, slithered
to vanish under vast waters.

Then we remembered Noah, took to the ships
and could have filled them a thousand times.
Many were left; we dared not turn again,
but cast off in the storm, clutching our thin life-threads.

II

Waters boiled, throwing black breakers into
black sky, churning together in chaos.
Many ships were lost
as furious foam broke steel, shattered wood.
We gave up hope, clung together, struck dumb
under shrieking movement. We could not live,
acknowledged defeat.

Slowly light cracked clouds,
the wind's whip softened, fell limply
and spinning darkness toppled aside,
blurred contours hardened
to sea and striped sky.
A slow calm flowed over our minds:
we opened our eyes and lived again.

III

A month has passed since we saw
the last spire. Drowned bells drift down
to the silent funeral.
Only sea remains wherever we look,
as we fish daily for food.
Our stores will soon be finished.

Perhaps we shall find some resting place,
a peak of this sunken planet
uncovered, grass-green fingers thrusting
to sunlight, calling us back to safety.
When we shall press glad feet into earth,
dry rocks scratching salt skin, as we
scramble to land, ghosts of a drowned star,
to search for food, to sleep and wake and breed.
And humanity may survive as
a curiosity, while some
scaly gill-breathing god moves through great
waves, choosing fish to inherit the world.

Edwin Brock

Song of the Battery Hen

We can't grumble about accommodation:
we have a new concrete floor that's
always dry, four walls that are
painted white, and a sheet-iron roof
the rain drums on. A fan blows warm air
beneath our feet to disperse the smell
of chicken-shit and, on dull days,
fluorescent lighting sees us.

You can tell me: if you come by
the North Door, I am in the twelfth pen
on the left-hand side of the third row
from the floor; and in that pen
I am usually the middle one of three.
But even without directions, you'd
discover me. I have the same orange-
red comb, yellow beak and auburn
feathers; but as the door opens and you
hear above the electric fan a kind of
one-word wail, I am the one
who sounds loudest in my head.

185

Listen. Outside this house there's an
orchard with small moss-green apple
trees; beyond that, two fields of
cabbages; then, on the far side of
the road, a broiler-house. Listen:
one cockerel grows out of there, as
tall and proud as the first hour of sun.
Sometimes I stop calling with the others
to listen, and wonder if he hears me.

The next time you come here, look for me.
Notice the way I sound inside my head.
God made us all quite differently,
and blessed us with this expensive home.

Stewart Conn

Strange Seraph

A cart-horse clumps up Broughton Street,
Pounding the dun cobbles into themselves
With hooves like hammers that beat
Sparks where the causeway shelves

To the gutter. Carved head slung back,
Clamped mouth showing teeth, he reeks
Of effort. Smooth shoulders, black
And varnished, ply a rhythm that speaks

Its proven purpose. On his wide
Forehead, a star—with bright
Harness making horse strange seraph tied
To *here* and *now* by shafts of light.

A shoe skliffs. Partly thrown
Off balance he is jerked upright
By crupper and chain. Foam blown
Finely from nostrils wreathes his sight,

As he grapples to contemplate
White fields' more true environment,
With no thwacking coalman to berate
186 Him but what he himself would invent.

For this Edinburgh is to him
Neither garden city nor Elysium:
With nothing for it but to drag the dream
Along, he stamps and lets off clouds of steam.

John Fairfax

Beyond Astronaut

And out in the black chart
Of lightlives away ride the roaring
Boys who slide through space.

A universe of unmapped grief and love
And new master light is beyond
The pleiades and plough and southern stars.
Far sisters far behind, left standing
As lean lads gyrate, siren
Silent, through the bewildering sky.
See them take a superstition which makes
Endless the forever night of destiny
Beyond sight or measure.

        O soaring
Icarus of outworld, burn bright
The traceries of known skymarks,
Slide the highway planets behind
Your clear waxed wings.

Go conquer the everywhere left
Beyond your sad confinement
In a predicted bonehouse,
Witch thrown riddle of flesh
And water.

        O soar until nothing
Remains but great glittering holes
In the black godspun shirt over your head.

Bryn Griffiths

Singleton Pool

Here the water shimmers, distorts the web of things;
Glasses the mind's map of new thought
With the tracery of old memories:
The time of clear seasons in the child's unmarred pattern of sight,
The shallow pool's once fathomless dangers,
The days of safe fishing in changeless light.

And yet now the pool, once clear water,
Is logged with lily leaves; spreads a green face
Over green depths where now no dangers move
For the new children that fish and play here.
Just carp and roach twine under the anchored lilies.
Only spiders skid over the glass of still water,
Below the thrash of hovering birds.

But there's still a danger here, years waiting,
To be dredged from darkness—
There's still a danger dormant in the choked pool
And the mind's packed landscape . . .
Only the trigger of words holds back thought,
Contains the fear of a child forgotten summers ago.

Seamus Heaney

Follower

My father worked with a horse-plough,
His shoulders globed like a full sail strung
Between the shafts and the furrow.
The horses strained at his clicking tongue.

An expert. He would set the wing
And fit the bright steel-pointed sock.
The sod rolled over without breaking.
At the headrig, with a single pluck

Of reins, the sweating team turned round
And back into the land. His eye
Narrowed and angled at the ground,
188 Mapping the furrow exactly.

I stumbled in his hob-nailed wake,
Fell sometimes on the polished sod;
Sometimes he rode me on his back
Dipping and rising to his plod.

I wanted to grow up and plough,
To close one eye, stiffen my arm.
All I ever did was follow
In his broad shadow round the farm.

I was a nuisance, tripping, falling,
Yapping always. But today
It is my father who keeps stumbling
Behind me, and will not go away.

Geoffrey Holloway

To a Calf Born on Sunday

Most tender, most topical of clowns,
so helpless, even, that I cannot laugh
at your gawkiness, the way you stumble, flop
from knobbly sticks to flounder frantically,
then dazed, half-kneeling, try once more
with stilted rear-legs furiously to force
the silly pair in front to hold
one noble second quite conclusively . . .
unforgettable, you that entered on the world
head-in-hooves, as if your sudden birth
were an interruption of some praying silence,
here, now, observe your triumph and beatitude.

Soon, a time must intervene
whose wit's too practical for simpletons like you,
too near the marrow for the unassuming funnybone.
Soon it will be foot-rot, flies,
mists that suffocate, winds that drive,
derisive, through the sodden, serfmarked ear . . .
Soon—perhaps indifferently—we'll watch
you passing anonymously by:
a roulette of eyeballs rolled without a chance
round the bars of a tumbril systematically trailing
to oblivion: a gun, a gaudy slab . . .

But this, this is your day.
Rest, therefore, in its sensuous immediacies,
tributes to the birthday of an innocence
no less the genuine if brittle, short.
Admit your charities: the lush lather
of a new coat with its poignant match
of early primrose, mushroom-grey;
the rough relish of a mother's tongue
painting, repainting, every fleck;
the grove of elders gazing
chestnut-eyed at these immense antics;
and the earth, the ancient pedestal,
straightening your feet, your novice knees;
setting you, this day at least, foresquare;
the fool-prince of an unbearable felicity,
heaven-schooled, among the buttercups.

Michael Ivens

Haifa Bay in the Morning

I saw a ship come sailing in,
Sailing in, sailing in,
With a list like a stormtrooper's twisted grin
At Haifa Bay in the morning.

The Army boat was waiting there,
(Haganah flashed 'Take care! Take care!')
The amiable squaddies all a'stare
Just three miles out in the morning.

And I was there in my little press boat
With one stout Guardsman to keep it afloat
And a man from *The Times* who claimed he wrote
And a blasé photographer yawning.

Their lousy ship they bought from a Greek,
That it ever arrived was a flaming freak
Considering the size of its list and leak
Off Palestine in the morning.

Through shortage of water two girls had died
(Gone their dreams of a Sabra's bride),
But two young boys jumped over the side
190 As the troopship moved close in the morning.

They could see the coast of the Holy Land
And the beckoning gleam of Haifa's sand
And hoped for Haganah to give them a hand
To lose themselves in the morning.

But I was there with my little press launch
Full of zeal with my Guardsman staunch,
And when the two Zionists ceased to float
We hauled them up in our little press boat
And tried to explain they'd come to no harm.
(Both had numbers tattooed on their arms
In a quaint old Belsen warning.)

My Guardsman, a reprobate Irish Mick,
Albeit a lapsed Catholick,
Said, 'Give the poor devils a chance to run
And then we'll go back and face the fun.'
His Paddy's face white in the morning.

But the immigrant ship was towed to the quay
And the two little Zionists brought in by me;
One old Jew jumped over the side
And kissed the ground and cried and cried;
Another leapt down and split his head
And bled an Hebraic script of red
On the Holy Quay in the morning.

An Army troopship took them away
With swift discretion the very next day
And Haifa wept as they sailed away
To a Cyprus camp in the morning.

ENVOI

They all are back in Israel now
And the two young Zionists work at the plough,
And my stalwart drunken Irish Mick
Is a reformed much-married Catholick.
But my mind it goes back to Haifa Bay
And dwells on the words I dared not say
And the sorrowful ship that sailed away
From the Holy Land in the morning.

Michael Longley

Camouflage

Our towns decayed, our gardens overgrown,
Weather we lament, the ivy creeping—
No matter what the setting, we are shown
(Whose one peculiar knack is weeping)
To differ from the beasts because they own
Those landscapes with which they are in keeping.

The leopard's coat accepting light through leaves,
Giraffes whose necks presume that certain trees
Are tall, whose elongated stance relieves
Those boughs of height's responsibilities,—
Such attributes a balanced world conceives,
Itself reflected, its streams reflecting these.

We'd say they choose a mood to linger at:
Like white for weddings, black for funerals,
It turns to habit—then to habitat,
So deftly not a single one recalls
What he's exemplar of: more likely that
One long enlightened dawn these animals,

Betrayed by awkward mornings for an age,
By their furs and feathers long forsaken,
Put the usual scenery to advantage
But are nonetheless obliged to waken
(Amid the sanctuary of camouflage)
To a change of colour, a risk taken.

Derek Mahon

Bird Sanctuary

Towards sleep I came
Upon the place again—
Its paper sea and tame
Unpredatory wind. The rain
Falls only after dark, and then
Steams out to sea at dawn . . .

I have erected
A bird sanctuary, to hold
The loaded world in check.
This is where all my birds collect—
Cormorant, puffin and kittiwake
All duly enrolled.

I live elsewhere—
In a city down the coast
Composed of earth and fire.
At night I walk beside the river
So that the elements of air
And water are not lost.

I expect great things
Of these angels of wind,
Females, males and fledgelings.
The sudden whirring of their wings
Disturbs the noon, and midnight rings
With echoes of their island.

In the event of earthquake
Or scorched earth, we shall see
Their strange unkillability—
Cormorant, puffin and kittiwake
Rise on unloaded wings to make
This world their sanctuary.

Gerald Moore

Stranger

The moon brings drums.
When it is full noise floods the valleys
Like light, and the Englishman
Vacantly winds his watch;
Penned on the dark fringe
Of life he gropes for crumbs
Through the bars of his skin,
Like a stiff grown-up who suddenly wants to play
With children but has forgotten the way,
Or a child again, wakeful and hearty,
Imprisoned upstairs on the night of a party.

Gerald Moore

A Beggar

An old man crying
Comes through the garden
  He is afraid.
Why do I stiffen
Against his crying
And throw him money
  Without love?

I am constrained
Because he shows me
  His human need.
Money is easy
Picked from the gravel
And to throw pity
  Hard for us both.

The old man has given
More to this action
  Than righteousness.
He showed his need
And I my silver;
Is that why beggars
  Always embarrass?

Better to spurn him
With flow of feeling
And have the courage
To give him nothing,
Than cheat his claim
  And cheapen life
  With a show of coin.

Stewart Parker

Health

Is this God's joke? my father screamed,
Gripped by the fingers that sprouted and waggled
From the raw holes in my shoulders.
Why blame a God you can't believe in?

Is this the sin of a generation,
The work of hands that worked together
To annihilate hands? my mother cried.
But I blame no God or man or nation
For my grim disarmament.
Health is my ambition.

Each day, the tin arms swivel.
I tame them. I labour hard for grace, like a good
    guitarist when they swing and glide.
I am satisfied when I lift a cup to my face, or write my name.
What I fight is pride
In these small, humble conquests.
Who would be proud of a body?
There is only the daily struggle for peace, and
The search from day to day shared
Living, for
Life is abundant; life will not be squashed,
There is only the lifting of hands to shake hands
And the lifting of arms to embrace.

Paul Roche

A Paradigm of Love

Does love live
Only
As a mirror lives
And give
So much back
Only
As a mirror gives
Which gazes
Only
With what gazing gave
And gives
By gazing back—
That only?

Can love live
Only
As an echo lives
In places
Where a shout has called

195

And give
Back only
As an echo gives
Which falling
Faces only
On the back of calling
And gives by lack—
That only?

No. Love lives
More really
Than a mirror lives
Less ghostly
Than an echo gives
Back only
Shadows to a call
More deeply
Throws all
Its substance out
Can stun,
But sweetly
Less like an echo than a shout
Less like a shadow than the sun:
Not only
Dangerous
But lonely.

Jean Salisbury

The Cypriots

It's not the place I mean—
I have been there before,
Old Peabody Buildings
With darkness firmly wedged in on each floor,

Washing befuddling the chinks of day,
Echoes of children standing in the porch,
Doors lost in their dark green,
The rusty foliage on the heavy knocker—

It is the faces that I cherish
Gentled by the insufficient light;
The children sit, hands folded, on stiff chairs
Quiet with awe as if in some dim church.

They speak little English, speak it slow
Engrossed, it seems, in a deep piety
That wrinkles round their eyes a secret laughter,
Their greased black hair as slim as sacred wax.

Maria, Antoniou and Yiangos
Cannot do well at school this generation,
Will fit in where we most expect a stranger,
Will become machinists, barbers, waiters;

But in this crowded hovel they have managed
A silent bond of close-knit dignity,
Gathered round their mother who has carried
Grace from a quick and poor and sunlit country.

Joan Murray Simpson

Driving at Night

This necklace loosens one by one its pearls
That slide towards me, swallowed by the dark.
The dashboard moonclock tells the time of speed.
Small rattlings, the wind's rush, the engine's burr,
Enclose me in a safe cocoon of sound.
Beyond on either hand are furry trees
And dark and deep the sky so rarely seen
Without the glare of lightning. Shall I stop?
No duties claim, no promises prevent.
There would be stillness and wet grass and leaves,
The nutshell scent of autumn and the trees'
Live presences, the unimpeded sky . . .

Yet I rush on, compulsive, through the night,
Bemused by this bright stream of beads unstrung,
Brilliant as tracer bullets and as swift.
There must be time for standing under trees,
For gazing at the enigmatic sky;
But the man-made has beauty of its own,
Loving the past, I prize the present, too—
Aerodynamics and the clean streamline,
Sweeping, uncluttered planes of wood or stone,
Prospects of soaring glass open to view
And power of speed that bears me, core of light,
Through the unaltered darkness of the night.

197

Ian Crichton Smith

The Lone Rider

It's not the worst ones that things happen to.
Often across the countries of the mind
one sees the careless ones, carelessly riding through
a beautiful land, without dark cloud or wind,
almost like pictures ill luck can't pursue.

They laugh in taverns and they drink cool water,
they descend high mountains to the other side
in a curve of easiness language cannot utter,
they and the horses that they calmly ride
are quite inseparable in centaur weather.

But the others with their wagons all weighed down
by women's hysteria, furniture, design—
the Indians attack them, and at dawn
the wolves lope by them with their famished skin
shining a little in the morning's shine.

And finally they're cornered in a canyon
where the mountains rise around them. Water spent
and ammunition finished, they drive on,
lugging their wardrobes and their sweet sad scent.
A yellow light entombs the caravan

lit with bright flashes of the lone rider
who climbs the jagged mountains, and is still
one step ahead of wolves and Indian murder.
His tireless horse strides on. From hill to hill
they watch with love their thirsty soul's provider.

D. M. Thomas

The Day Before the Last

The soil was tougher, stonier to the spade
In the new-broken field, and so he laboured
Long into evening. The air turned cold;
His hands ached, and he'd missed a favourite programme.
No angel came
To tell him this was unneeded, pointless work

—For all his holy trade—that he might have rested.
And now the expensive earth stood piled high.

Over this earth, and over the spilled churchyard
The sun was setting, as it always had—
Shedding a peaceful, ordinary light
On the closed community of simple graves.
Nothing to tell. Nothing to tell the world
This was the end, the very last of its sunsets;
And the new field in vain.

If there was a sign, if we had only known
On that brown-eyed day in September
(Not yet the end of British Summer Time)
That time itself was a departing guest,
We'd have cried in the streets, and faltered tears of passion,
To see the crimson go out of the last sky . . .
If we had known, we'd surely have done *something*.
Instead, we drank our coffee and went upstairs,
And said a prayer by rote perhaps—and slept.
The day had been—you understand?—so normal,
And so tomorrow would be. Nothing said:
'No more the spade to earth, the hand to plough;
This is the twilight Eden, more endeared
By human love, and its most precious dust.'

W. Price Turner

Didacticism as a Kind of Prism

To paint moustaches on the Mona Lisa
is an act of vandalism. It is also
criticism, embodying a point of view.

Is the practice of criticism, then
a form of vandalism, a mask beneath
which festers a vicious wish, or do

all vandals subconsciously desire
perfection? Is a compulsion to erase
just intolerance for the trivial untrue?

Can I possibly be the same person, being
father, son and wholly gauche as I begin
to separate my selves? I wish I knew.

199

The lantern-fly fools some of the critics
some of the time with his mask on a stick
held high in jaunty camouflage, but who

knows what gourmets will go for next, or
where maggots get to when apples rot . . .
Study the patrons of the X-film queue.

All that impoverished eagerness, senile
or green, is fellow-feeling, loneliness
for ogres that we never quite outgrew.

I think of brains pickled in jars, arrested
development, the pale chap with the duster
coughing back chalk at his black bored crew.

Once leeches were the universal cure-alls;
now we slap on these academic murals,
stuck for progressive ways to misconstrue.

Progress, like all passions, remains relative
to what is expedient, what vital,
and how much blood one cares to wade through.

W. Price Turner

Fable from Life

Eight hundred telephone directories
will bulletproof a truck, claims
a fruit company in South America.
Think of a bullet with so many numbers
on it, stopping nothing. Bandits
clamped to their rocks like wild posies,
leap up, banging and screeching.
The desert bristles with rifles
and vexed moustaches. After all
that fuss, the truck bumps on.
Fruitless compliments to the Patron Saint
of Tough Luck, then a clutter of big hats
raises a thin oasis of ritual smoke.
El Moroso, who once broke a tooth
on his own bullet in the first bite
of cool plunder, savours the loss.
The moral is clearly to have no truck
with thick-skinned civilisations.

Ivan White

The Tempered Theft

Excavate here.
    Most recesses are dumb—
Often declare
    Nothing to those who come
Prospecting near
    A dead king's disguised tomb.

Loose canker shifts
    Revealing the first signs.
A dry must wafts
    From soil; soon our lust cranes
Over the crafts
    Unearthed as the spade mines.

Instinct proved true.
    He reclines here untied
Of flesh; the few
    Strands of his clothes powdered
In air as though
    Light ripped his bones naked.

Much to excite
    Us, small trinkets—his need
For things in sight
    After death; their envied
Substance, goldbright,
    That he feared to discard.

Eyeholes grimace
    Under his skull's facade,
Through which abuse
    Some past decadence strayed
From his demise
    To acknowledge our greed.

Raymond Wilson

Escape

At first, collusion mumbled in the dark,
A sentry coughing somewhere in the cold,

With searchlights ranging, opening up like fans
(Cracked walls—ranged beds) and closing, fold on fold.

Next the elaborate deceit by day,
Grotesque charades of innocence, a blind
Man's buff of whistled danger, panic cough,
Sudden disaster in a scratched behind.

It seemed so easy, since beyond all doubt
The enemy was dull as he was vile:
How could the merely brutal storm our dreams,
The crassly ignorant outwit our guile?

Meanwhile, the tunnel, womb to our despair,
Grew granite to the touch, broke man by man
The best of us (the worst as usual sneered,
Abandoning all interest in the plan).

At last just one, who dug for digging's sake,
Hunched in the hot vomit of his fear,
Through slit eyes, acid with his stinging sweat,
Laboured a dream from granite, saw appear

Day, that ran crumbling at his finger-tips,
Light spilling to the grave like grains of sand,
Air sweet as syrup, and the green earth's roots—
Aspiring harvest—cradled in his hand.

Tom Wright

Frontier Guard

The barbed wire is erected and the guns deployed.
The guard patrols with winter's lead weighting his feet
and darkness is his enemy as it is mine.
The rifle on his shoulder could hail out my death
or summon his should he forget I did not call him
from his warm moonfaced Ninotchka
to the checkpoint where the wind ignores his challenge
and makes free with zones and frontiers,
and ice aches along his veins.
The darkness is our mutual foe. My stiff bones groan
and grumble as the cold salts my old wounds and his.

And my Ninotchka is no nearer;
she would weep as much should I personify my hate
in him and blaze it on the deadness of the night.

I could call out to him as brother, tovarich,
or friend; tell him I too have crucified my God,
and have been crucified, that what he hates I hate,
or simply that the darkness is our enemy.
But he would only hear an ambush in my voice.
For we are isolated and expendable,
making our separate tracks on the same snow,
divided, conquered by the dark that seals us in.
Ice smokes our breath with malice and the trumpet tongue
of fear musters a monster up behind the wire,
and I am his monster as he is mine.

We, whom our common isolation should unite,
stamp, blow, but cannot generate a common thaw,
nor furnish common law to meet our common cause,
nor wrest a common summer from the earth.
The ice attacks us and the darkness separates.
Only our challenge dares to cross the frontier line.

Douglas Livingstone

Fringes

Not a sparrow falls
not even at the derelict dumping-site,
on the outskirts of town.

A curlew calls
in sleep far up the river where night
slips off her dressing gown.

The mudflats hump
in the warm lagoon's disgorging jaws;
crying, the gulls sail in.

Dawn fans the sump
of civilisation where the outlaws
shack up in shanties of tin.

Too early yet
for the shrimp-diggers, the quietening
of the all-night sea.

The sun, still wet,
pauses below its bunched brightening,
only the gulls have it free.

Douglas Livingstone

Flood

Ut-Napashtim, after dark,
in sly communion with the gods,
well-forewarned on all the odds,
built himself a wooden ark;

rounded up the bridling pairs
of donkeys, sheep, bar-striped zebra,
lions, panthers, goats, etc.
from deserts and their mountain lairs;

cooped them in a stuffy hold,
made his plans for thirst and food,
kept the peace with curses rude
and ample straw to pad the cold;

collected samples of the times:
chairs and papyrus and cloth,
carven gods, benign and wrath,
copies of his favourite rhymes;

with blows and proddings got his train
of testy relatives aboard,
locked the bins where the drinks were stored
and sat and waited for the rain.

Alan McLean

July: After Fires

Valley and hill hold
Ricketty trees whittled by bushfires;
Especially proteas, flowers all singed
By what covered the ground with ashes.
Greying a little, they washed at your shoes
And drift like charred sand.
Landscapes lie open, stripped; from hills
Seem to float away to the edge of a sky
That always waits for their end.
Yet look close among this waste
Green shoots already pierce the earth
In thousands. A host
Of what will be saplings, then real trees,
At last, when inevitable flames reach them
This time next year, fine dust
Of dead, life-giving ashes.

Alan McLean

African Discovery

Did I find it beautiful now?
You asked, pointing from the top of a hill
We'd slogged up to through rocks
And thorns and weak-kneed trees,
Socks and trousers quilled with blackjacks
(it was April).
        Yes—looking down
On that firebreak rolling stolidly over hills
Matted identical to ours—Yes, I said.
For at last these headless humps,
The bushfires smoke-signalling the start of winter,
That far-off sheen of water, all seemed to mean
A beginning to beauty. Or was it,
As the voices reaching from an unseen village
Had it, more a change in me
Seizing this moment for fruition?

Acknowledgements

For permission to reproduce poems in this book the Editor and publishers are indebted to the poets and to the following:

Angus & Robertson (Sydney) for 'Windy Gap' by David Campbell, taken from *The Miracle of Mullion Hill* and for 'Going to Sleep' by Chris Wallace-Crabbe, taken from *In Light and Darkness.*

The Asia Society for *The Smell of Mankind* by N. M. Rashed.

Jonathan Cape Ltd., for 'The Glory Trumpeter' by Derek Walcott, taken from *The Castaway.*

F. W. Cheshire Ltd., (Melbourne), for 'How to Go On Not Looking' and 'Abandonment of Autos' by Bruce Dawe, taken from *A Need of a Similar Name* and for 'Noah's Song' by Evan Jones taken from *Inside the Whale.*

J. M. Dent & Sons Ltd., for 'Singleton Pool' by Bryn Griffiths, taken from *The Stones Remember.*

Andre Deutsch, Ltd., for 'An Old Jamaican Woman thinks about the Hereafter' and 'Challenge' by A. L. Hendriks, taken from *On This Mountain.*

Eyre & Spottiswoode Ltd., for 'The Lone Rider' by Ian Crichton Smith, taken from *The Law and The Grace.*

The Hand & Flower Press for 'Andromache' by Patrick Fernando taken from *The Return of Ulysses.*

David Higham Associates for 'The Meaning of Africa' by Abioseh Nicol.

Jacaranda Press, Ltd., (Brisbane) for 'Water Skier' by Thomas W. Shapcott, taken from *Time on Fire.*

Longmans, Green & Co. Ltd., for 'Akibu', 'Night Rain' and 'Flight Across Africa' by John Pepper Clark, taken from *A Reed and Tide.*

McClelland & Stewart Ltd., (Ontario) for 'On Hearing a Name Long Unspoken' by Leonard Cohen, taken from *Flowers for Hitler.*

Oxford University Press, Ltd., for 'A Caged Beast' by Edward Lucie-Smith, taken from *Confessions and Histories,* and for 'The Fall' by A. K. Ramanujan, taken from *The Striders.*

Oxford University Press, Ltd., (Malaya) for 'Embers' by A. Samad Said, taken from *Modern Malay Verse 1946-61.*

Pegasus Press, Ltd., (New Zealand) for 'Parade: Liberation Day' by Kevin Ireland and for 'After the Rocket's Blast' by J. E. Weir, taken from *The Sudden Sun.*

The Spectator, for 'The Tempered Theft' by Ivan White.

University London Press, Ltd., for 'After the Holocaust' and 'Apocalypse at Birth' by Frank Kobina Parkes, taken from *Songs of the Wilderness.*

Whilst every effort has been made to trace the owners of copyrights. In a few cases this has proved impossible, and we take this opportunity of tendering our apologies to any owners whose rights may have been unwittingly infringed.